TEACHING STUDENTS
WITH
SENSORY DISABILITIES

A PRACTICAL APPROACH TO SPECIAL EDUCATION FOR EVERY TEACHER

The Fundamentals of Special Education
A Practical Guide for Every Teacher

The Legal Foundations of Special Education
A Practical Guide for Every Teacher

Effective Assessment for Students With Special Needs
A Practical Guide for Every Teacher

Effective Instruction for Students With Special Needs
A Practical Guide for Every Teacher

Working With Families and Community Agencies to Support Students With Special Needs
A Practical Guide for Every Teacher

Public Policy, School Reform, and Special Education
A Practical Guide for Every Teacher

Teaching Students With Sensory Disabilities
A Practical Guide for Every Teacher

Teaching Students With Medical, Physical, and Multiple Disabilities
A Practical Guide for Every Teacher

Teaching Students With Learning Disabilities
A Practical Guide for Every Teacher

Teaching Students With Communication Disorders
A Practical Guide for Every Teacher

Teaching Students With Emotional Disturbance
A Practical Guide for Every Teacher

Teaching Students With Mental Retardation
A Practical Guide for Every Teacher

Teaching Students With Gifts and Talents
A Practical Guide for Every Teacher

TEACHING STUDENTS
WITH
SENSORY DISABILITIES

A Practical Guide for Every Teacher

BOB ALGOZZINE
JIM YSSELDYKE

CORWIN PRESS
A SAGE Publications Company
Thousand Oaks, California

For information:

Corwin Press
A Sage Publications Company
2455 Teller Road
Thousand Oaks, California 91320
www.corwinpress.com

Sage Publications Ltd.
1 Oliver's Yard
55 City Road
London EC1Y 1SP
United Kingdom

Sage Publications India Pvt. Ltd.
B-42, Panchsheel Enclave
Post Box 4109
New Delhi 110 017 India

Printed in the United States of America

Library of Congress Cataloging-in-Publication Data

Algozzine, Robert.
Teaching students with sensory disabilities: A practical guide for every teacher / Bob Algozzine and James E. Ysseldyke.
    p. cm.
Includes bibliographical references and index.
ISBN 1-4129-3947-X (cloth)
ISBN 1-4129-3900-3 (pbk.)
    1. Children with disabilities—Education. 2. Sensory disorders in children. I. Ysseldyke, James E. II. Title.
LC4015.A52 2006
371.91'1—dc22

                                                        2005037823

This book is printed on acid-free paper.

06 07 08 09 10 9 8 7 6 5 4 3 2 1

Acquisitions Editor:	Kylee M. Liegl
Editorial Assistant:	Nadia Kashper
Production Editor:	Denise Santoyo
Copy Editor:	Karen E. Taylor
Typesetter:	C&M Digitals (P) Ltd.
Indexer:	Kathy Paparchontis
Cover Designer:	Michael Dubowe

Contents

About
A Practical Approach to Special Education for Every Teacher

*S*pecial education means specially designed instruction for students with unique learning needs. Students receive special education for many reasons. Students with disabilities such as mental retardation, hearing impairments (including deafness), speech or language impairments, visual impairments (including blindness), emotional disturbance, orthopedic impairments, autism, traumatic brain injury, other health impairments, or specific learning disabilities are entitled to special education services. Students who are gifted and talented also receive special education. Special education services are delivered in many settings, including regular classes, resource rooms, and separate classes. The 13 books of this collection will help you teach students with disabilities and those with gifts and talents. Each book focuses on a specific area of special education and can be used individually or in conjunction with all or some of the other books. Six of the books provide the background and content knowledge you need in order to work effectively with all students with unique learning needs:

Book 1: The Fundamentals of Special Education

Book 2: The Legal Foundations of Special Education

Book 3: Effective Assessment for Students With Special Needs

Book 4: Effective Instruction for Students With Special Needs

Book 5: Working With Families and Community Agencies to Support Students With Special Needs

Book 6: Public Policy, School Reform, and Special Education

Seven of the books focus on teaching specific groups of students who receive special education:

Book 7:   Teaching Students With Sensory Disabilities

Book 8:   Teaching Students With Medical, Physical, and Multiple Disabilities

Book 9:   Teaching Students With Learning Disabilities

Book 10: Teaching Students With Communication Disorders

Book 11: Teaching Students With Emotional Disturbance

Book 12: Teaching Students With Mental Retardation

Book 13: Teaching Students With Gifts and Talents

All of the books in *A Practical Approach to Special Education for Every Teacher* will help you to make a difference in the lives of all students, especially those with unique learning needs.

ACKNOWLEDGMENTS

The approach we take in *A Practical Approach to Special Education for Every Teacher* is an effort to change how professionals learn about special education. The 13 separate books are a result of prodding from our students and from professionals in the field to provide a set of materials that "cut to the chase" in teaching them about students with disabilities and about building the capacity of systems to meet those students' needs. Teachers told us that in their classes they always confront students with special learning needs and students their school district has assigned a label to (e.g., students with learning disabilities). Our students and the professionals we worked with wanted a very practical set of texts that gave them the necessary **information** *about* **the students** (e.g., federal definitions, student characteristics) and specific **information on** *what to do about* **the students** (assessment and teaching strategies, approaches that work). They also wanted the opportunity to purchase parts of textbooks, rather than entire texts, to learn what they needed.

The production of this collection would not have been possible without the support and assistance of many colleagues. Professionals associated with Corwin Press—Faye Zucker, Kylee Liegl, Robb Clouse—helped us work through the idea of introducing special education differently, and their support in helping us do it is deeply appreciated.

Faye Ysseldyke and Kate Algozzine, our children, and our grandchildren also deserve recognition. They have made the problems associated with the project very easy to diminish, deal with, or dismiss. Every day in every way, they enrich our lives and make us better. We are grateful for them.

About the Authors

Bob Algozzine, PhD, is Professor in the Department of Educational Leadership at the University of North Carolina at Charlotte and project codirector of the U.S. Department of Education–supported Behavior and Reading Improvement Center. With 25 years of research experience and extensive firsthand knowledge of teaching students classified as seriously emotionally disturbed (and other equally useless terms), Algozzine is a uniquely qualified staff developer, conference speaker, and teacher of behavior management and effective teaching courses.

As an active partner and collaborator with professionals in the Charlotte-Mecklenburg schools in North Carolina and as an editor of several journals focused on special education, Algozzine keeps his finger on the pulse of current special education practice. He has written more than 250 manuscripts on special education topics, authoring many popular books and textbooks on how to manage emotional and social behavior problems. Through *A Practical Approach to Special Education for Every Teacher,* Algozzine hopes to continue to help improve the lives of students with special needs—and the professionals who teach them.

Jim Ysseldyke, PhD, is Birkmaier Professor in the Department of Educational Psychology, director of the School Psychology Program, and director of the Center for Reading Research at the University of Minnesota. Widely requested as a staff developer and conference speaker, he brings more than 30 years of research and teaching experience to educational professionals around the globe.

As the former director of the federally funded National Center on Educational Outcomes, Ysseldyke conducted research and provided technical support that helped to boost the academic performance of students with disabilities and improve school assessment techniques nationally. Today he continues to work to improve the education of students with disabilities.

The author of more than 300 publications on special education and school psychology, Ysseldyke is best known for his textbooks on assessment, effective instruction, issues in special education, and other cutting-edge areas of education and school psychology. With *A Practical Approach to Special Education for Every Teacher*, he seeks to equip educators with practical knowledge and methods that will help them to better engage students in exploring—and meeting—all their potentials.

Self-Assessment 1

Before you begin this book, check your knowledge of the content being covered. Choose the best answer for each of the following questions.

1. The term that refers to all degrees of vision loss is

    a. visual impairments

    b blind

    c. legally blind

    d. deaf and blind

2. A _____ problem may make it difficult to see things clearly in the central visual field but relatively easy in the peripheral field.

    a. field of vision

    b. low vision

    c. visual acuity

    d. visual directive

3. Myopia, a term that describes the phenomenon of distant objects being blurry while close objects are in focus, is commonly called

    a. ocular motility

    b. nearsightedness

    c. astigmatism

    d. strabismus

4. Problems that affect the eyes' ability to move smoothly and focus properly refer to

   a. ocular motility

   b. farsightedness

   c. astigmatism

   d. nystagmus

5. During the past ten years, the number of students provided special education services because of visual impairments has

   a. increased

   b. remained constant

   c. decreased

   d. decreased and then increased

6. The term that refers to all degrees of hearing loss is

   a. sensory disorders

   b. deaf

   c. hard-of-hearing

   d. hearing impairments

7. Hearing loss that prevents the understanding of speech through the ear, with or without a hearing aid, is called

   a. hard-of-hearing

   b. deafness

   c. deaf and blind

   d. mild hearing loss

8. Auditory acuity is measure through

   a. intensity and frequency

   b. intensity and hertz

   c. frequency and decibels

   d. decibels and intensity

9. Loudness is measured in

   a. sound waves

   b. decibels

   c. hertz

   d. avis

10. A widely recognized sign language that uses both manual and other movements is called

   a. Original Sign Language

   b. Cued Speech

   c. Manual Speech and Language

   d. American Sign Language

REFLECTION

After you answer the multiple-choice questions, think about how you would answer the following questions:

- What factors might affect the academic success of individuals with visual impairments?
- What factors might affect the academic success of individuals with hearing impairments?
- What do effective teachers do to provide support for students with visual and hearing impairments?

Introduction to Teaching Students With Sensory Disabilities

"I'm going to be a lawyer—I'm supposed to read the fine print. What a joke. I can't even read the large print." **Mary** is legally blind and uses special equipment to help her read legal documents at the George Washington University Law Library.

"I love softball. I'm hitting .425, and my kids think I'm a sports hero. I guess I am." **Tommy** doesn't see well, but special adaptations like softballs with beepers and a closed-circuit television system help him lead a life much like his neighbors and peers.

"To be honest, we were concerned about placing **Pat** in the public school, but we couldn't be happier. It hasn't been a 'piece of cake,' but everything looks very promising right now." Pat was born blind. Kindergarten could have been a major problem, but mobility and listening-skills training made the transition from a special education preschool program to her neighborhood school go smoothly.

"When I think about all the things that could be wrong with me, I think I'm pretty lucky. I've had a great time in

(Continued)

(Continued)

high school, and I'm going to college with my best friend. Right now, that's all I want." **Sandy** is deaf. An interpreter uses sign language to communicate what is spoken by others and to let them know what Sandy has to say. A telecommunication device for the deaf (TDD) connected to the phone enables Sandy to make and receive calls.

"Ya know, growing up with **Barry** was just like growing up with Bobby. They both were royal pains. Hey, boys will be boys, and sometimes they will be your brothers." Barry is hard-of-hearing, and his sister learned sign language and finger spelling, so she can have private and public conversations with him.

People like Mary, Tommy, Pat, Sandy, and Barry receive special education because they have difficulty seeing and hearing. Of the five senses, seeing and hearing are most important for translating external information to traditional learning. People who have difficulty seeing or hearing have sensory disabilities referred to as visual impairments or hearing impairments. The term **visual impairments** refers to all degrees of vision loss. The term **hearing impairments** refers to all degrees of hearing loss. **Deafness and blindness** refers to a combination of hearing and visual impairments.

1

What Should Every Teacher Know About Visual Impairments?

Students with visual impairments were among the first to receive special education services in the United States (Fazzi & Pogrund, 2002; Orr & Rogers, 2002). The first institutional programs—the New England Asylum for the Blind and the New York Institution for the Blind—began in 1832. Five years later, the first residential school for students who were blind opened in Ohio. It was not until 1900 that the first day-school classes for students with visual impairments were held in Chicago, IL. In 1911, New York became the first state to make education compulsory for children with vision problems. In 1913, both Boston, MA, and Cleveland, OH, started classes for students who were partially sighted. Until the passage of the Education for All Handicapped Children Act (Public Law 94-142) in 1975, it was common to place students with visual impairments in residential settings and day schools. Today, more and more students with sensory disabilities are being included in general education classes with their neighbors and peers and are leading more productive lives, both in and out of school, as a result of it.

DEFINITION

According to U.S. federal regulations, a **visual impairment** is a problem seeing that, even with correction, adversely affects a child's educational performance. The term does not include people with normal or near-normal vision, but does include people with low visual functioning as well as those who have only light perception or those who are totally without the sense of vision (Barraga & Erin, 1992; Orr & Rogers, 2002). People with normal or near-normal vision can perform tasks without special assistance. People with low vision may have difficulty with detailed visual tasks or may perform them at reduced levels of speed, endurance, or accuracy, even with assistance. People who are blind or near-blind have unreliable vision and rely primarily or exclusively on other senses.

Visual impairments are often defined in terms of **visual acuity**—the ability to see things at specified distances. Visual acuity usually is measured by having the person read letters or discriminate objects at a distance of 20 feet. Those who are able to read the letters correctly have normal vision. Visual acuity is expressed as a ratio, which tells us how well the individual sees. The expression **20/20 vision** describes perfect (normal) vision; it means that the person can see at 20 feet what people with normal vision see at 20 feet. A person with 20/90 vision needs to be 20 feet away to discriminate letters or objects that a person with normal vision can read or discriminate at 90 feet.

How poor does visual acuity have to be in order to be considered a visual impairment? To address this question, the American Medical Association (AMA) adopted a definition of blindness in 1934 that is still used today and is included in federal law. According to that definition, the criterion for **blindness** is

> . . . central visual acuity of 20/200 or less in the better eye with corrective glasses or central visual acuity of more than 20/200 if there is a visual field defect in which the peripheral field is contracted to such an extent that the widest diameter of the visual field subtends an angular distance no greater than 20 degrees in the better eye. (Koestler, 1976, p. 45)

A person who needs to stand at a distance of 20 feet to see what a person with normal vision can see from 200 feet away is considered **legally blind**. The second part of the AMA definition is included so that people with a severely restricted field of vision are also considered legally blind. When looking straight ahead, a person with a **normal field of vision** is able to see objects within a range of approximately 180 degrees. Mary's field of vision is only 10 degrees, so she is able to see only a limited area at any one time, even though her visual acuity in that area is actually quite good. People with restricted visual fields sometimes liken the process of seeing to looking through a narrow tube or tunnel. Other field-of-vision problems make it difficult to see things clearly in the central visual field even though things can be seen relatively easily in the peripheral field.

ELIGIBILITY FOR SPECIAL EDUCATION

Students with blindness are not the only ones eligible for special education services. Students who have a visual impairment but are not blind (i.e., those with low vision) are also eligible. These are students with visual acuity greater than 20/200 but not greater than 20/70 in the better eye with correction. For most practical purposes, a student with a **visual impairment** is one who has visual acuity with correction of less than 20/70. In all cases, the standard is employed "with correction." This phrase means that, if the condition can be corrected with glasses or contact lenses, the student is not eligible for special education services.

Focusing Difficulties

Although the most frequently mentioned visual impairments are related to visual acuity and field of vision, how people see can also be affected by other problems. **Myopia**, or nearsightedness, is a condition in which people see objects that are close but not those at a distance. **Hyperopia**, or farsightedness, is a condition in which people see objects at a distance but not those that are close. **Astigmatism** is a condition in which the eyes produce images that are not equally in focus. **Ocular motility** problems affect the eyes' ability to move smoothly and focus properly. **Strabismus** describes an inability to focus both eyes on the same object, causing one eye to become nonfunctional and vision to be affected. **Nystagmus** is rapid, involuntary lateral, vertical, or rotary movements of the eye(s) that interfere with bringing objects into focus. Although conditions like nearsightedness, farsightedness, and astigmatism can affect school performance, they are most often corrected before or during school and are generally not considered visual impairments requiring special education services.

Visual Functioning

In recent years, teachers have begun to place more emphasis on visual functioning than on visual acuity or field of vision as measured by vision tests. This shift in focus takes into account that all students who are blind or who have low vision are not alike in the ways they use their vision. It is more common now for students with blindness or low vision to be classified in terms of the kinds of special assistance they need to be successful or the kinds of instructional approaches that are effective. From this perspective, students who are blind are those who must be educated through channels other than sight (using braille or audiotapes, for example). Students with low vision can use print materials, but may need modifications such as enlarged print or low-vision aids (magnification).

PREVALENCE

During recent school years, about 26,000 students with visual impairments received special education services; also in recent years, the proportion of students with visual impairments who have received services has decreased notably, by about 12 percent (U. S. Department of Education, 1993, 1999, 2000, 2001, 2002). This group represents about 0.05 percent of school-age children and adolescents and about 0.5 percent of students with disabilities. There is relatively little variation in the percentage of students identified in each of the states. In recent years, students with visual impairments had the second highest (48 percent) placement in general education classes; 20 percent were served from 21 to 60% outside general education classrooms, 17 percent were served more than 60% outside general education classrooms, and the remaining students were in separate school settings (U. S. Department of Education, 2000, 2001, 2002).

What You May See in Your Classroom

Students with visual impairments receive special education because their vision after correction remains limited to such an extent that it affects their development and achievement without intervention (Fazzi & Pogrund, 2002; Orr & Rogers, 2002; Peavey & Leff, 2002). Some possible signs of vision impairments are presented in Table1.1. Not being able to see as well as neighbors and peers may result in a variety of cognitive, academic, physical, behavioral, and communication characteristics if appropriate modification and specialized instructional interventions are not provided.

Cognitive Characteristics

Cognition is largely a matter of developing concepts. Because many concepts are learned entirely through visual means, students with visual impairments have difficulty learning some concepts. Think for a minute about the difficulty of learning concepts such as orange, circle, bigger, perpendicular, bright, and foggy with limited vision. Students who have visual impairments are not necessarily intellectually slower than their peers, but they may perform poorly on standard intelligence tests (Orr & Rogers, 2002). The reason? The nature of those tests. Look at the following items from intelligence tests:

Table 1.1   Top Ten Signs of Visual Impairments

---

1. Student frequently experiences watery eyes.

2. Student frequently experiences red or inflamed eyes.

3. Student's eye movements are jumpy or not synchronized.

4. Student experiences difficulty moving around the classroom.

5. Student experiences difficulty reading small print.

6. Student experiences difficulty identifying small details in pictures or illustrations.

7. Student frequently complains of dizziness after reading a passage or completing an assignment involving vision.

8. Student tilts head or squints eyes to achieve better focus.

9. Student uses one eye more than the other for reading or completing other assignments.

10. Student frequently complains of headaches or eye infections.

What is a collar?

What is a pagoda?

Tell me another word for *illuminate?*

In what way are a radio tower and a police car alike?

Clearly, prior visual information is helpful in providing answers to questions like these. Similarly, many subtests and items on intelligence tests require that students see the stimuli and responses: Students are shown pictures and asked to identify them; they are shown bead patterns and asked to reproduce them; they are shown visual stimulus arrays and asked to find the one stimulus that differs from the others. Performances on test items like these are greatly influenced by how well students see.

Academic Characteristics

Newland (1986) reported that "with the exception of unique problems of input and possibly a greater demand in processing, the fundamental learning procedures of blind children do not differ from those of nonimpaired children" (p. 576). The impact of visual impairments on academic performance is very much a function of the severity of the condition (i.e., the degree of vision loss and its causes) and the age at which the student's vision was reduced. Modifications for students should be determined individually using assessment data; they should not be based simply on vision status classification. With appropriate assistance, students with visual impairments achieve academic success just like their neighbors and peers without visual impairments (Orr & Rogers, 2002).

The academic needs of students with visual impairments reflect a dual curriculum perspective that consists of

Traditional academic content that is the same as that taught to peers, and

Disability-specific content needed to be successful in the traditional curriculum.

Disability-specific skills include those related to concept development and communication, such as braille reading and writing, listening skills, use of a slate and stylus, use of an abacus for math, handwriting, and keyboarding. Additional skills may also be needed to enable the student to access the traditional curriculum (e.g., tactual map-reading skills). Access technology may also be necessary, including speech and braille access devices commonly known as screen readers and refreshable braille.

Meeting the academic needs of students with low vision frequently requires modifications to the environment and instructional materials as well as special equipment that will enhance a student's ability to acquire print information. Environmental modifications such as additional lighting and special seating arrangements may be required. Material modifications (such as adapting print materials to promote maximum contrast, minimal visual distractions, and special size requirements) may be necessary. Equipment and assistive technology that provides access to print information may be needed (e.g., magnifiers, closed-circuit television, and telescopic aids).

For young students, skills that emphasize the use of vision may require attention. Teaching modifications may be necessary, including allowing more time for completion of assignments and tests and providing shorter blocks of time for extensive reading assignments in order to prevent fatigue. Reducing the amount of copy work and drill work assignments (if concepts are understood) may help students produce quality products. Narration of videos and other visually presented information that is shown at a distance may facilitate information acquisition along with verbalizing writing on the chalkboard or overhead projector.

Physical Characteristics

In terms of size and appearance, people with visual impairments are no different from those with normal vision (Orr & Rogers, 2002). As children develop, however, low vision and blindness may impact movement and the quality of motor skills. Imitation from visual observations, a primary method of learning for young children, may be absent for the child with a visual disability. In addition, information acquired through "incidental learning" (unintended learning through observation) may be unavailable to a child with a visual disability. Some children with visual difficulties also develop repetitive stereotypic movements commonly referred to as "blindisms," such as rocking, eye poking, head rolling, and hand waving.

Instruction in nonacademic, disability-specific skills that encourage appropriate physical growth and independence begins in early childhood and continues throughout a student's schooling. Emphasis on orientation and mobility is an essential component of the curriculum and should be available to every student with a visual impairment. **Orientation** refers to the ability to know where one is in relation to the environment. **Mobility** is the ability to move safely and efficiently from one place to another. Activities that provide and promote movement may discourage undesirable behaviors such as blindisms. A curriculum that includes and emphasizes nonacademic, disability-specific skills will enable a student to develop more fully.

Behavioral Characteristics

In general, there are few social and emotional characteristics specific to students with visual disabilities (D'Allura, 2002;

Peavey & Leff, 2002). However, low vision and blindness may influence behavior. Nonacademic skills that may be affected include social skills, affective understanding, and nonverbal or body language behavior. In addition, independence in all areas of development will affect a student's behavior and the behavior of others toward the student.

Social skills are important to a student's overall success. Students need instruction and feedback in appropriate ways of interacting with others such as initiating a conversation without eye contact, age-appropriate ways of sitting and standing, and facial expressions. Many students with visual impairments cannot see nonverbal forms of communication, so they miss out on the information and feelings displayed with a look, a nod, a smile, a frown, or a shrug.

Students with visual impairments can be taught to assert themselves from an early age to maintain and develop age-appropriate independence. It is important for students with disabilities to learn from their peers without disabilities. For developing healthy self-concepts, it is equally important that they learn from peers and role models with visual disabilities. Meeting behavioral needs of students with visual disabilities works best not in isolation but in the environments in which the behaviors naturally occur.

Communication Characteristics

Communication is the primary area in which students with visual impairments experience difficulty (Orr & Rogers, 2002). To read, for example, they sometimes have to use large-print books, special reading methods (braille), or recorded materials and readers. Many students with visual impairments are able to use special optical devices, such as magnifiers, small telescopes, glasses, or contact lenses to help them perform better at tasks such as reading. Most teachers find that students with visual impairments prefer reading regular print with the assistance of an optical device rather than large-print materials (Corn & Ryser, 1989).

To be successful, students with visual impairments require interventions that help them make up for their loss of vision (Chang & Schaller, 2002; Orr & Rogers, 2002). Some general interventions for students with vision impairments are presented in Table 1.2.

Table 1.2   Top Ten Tips for Teachers of Students With Visual Impairments

1. Reduce the distance between the student and speaker as much as possible.

2. Reduce glare and visual distractions as much as possible.

3. Reduce clutter on classroom floor and provide unobstructed access to the door and to key classroom spaces.

4. Seat the student near the chalkboard or overhead projections.

5. Avoid partially opening cabinets, storage areas, and classroom doors; fully opened or closed doors are safer.

6. Use complete sentences to provide additional context during conversations or instructional presentations.

7. Use auditory cues when referring to objects in the classroom and during instructional presentations.

8. Reduce unnecessary noise to help the student focus on the content of instructional presentations.

9. Keep instructional materials in a consistent, specific place so the student knows where to find them easily.

10. Make sure eyeglasses and other visual aids are functioning properly.

Critical to the literacy needs of students with visual impairments is determining an appropriate literacy medium. This determination should be based on an assessment of individual communication and learning skills. The decision to use braille or print (or a combination) for reading and writing may be obvious for a student who is totally blind, but it can be a difficult decision for a student with low vision. A sampling of factors that assist teachers in making this decision includes a student's preferences in using vision or touch to complete tasks, degree of vision, ability to read his or her own handwriting, fatigue, as well as the presence of other disabilities. In addition, the use of large-print and auditory materials and tools should be based on a thorough and ongoing media assessment. Most teachers find that students with visual impairments prefer reading regular print with the assistance of an optical reader rather than reading large-print materials.

2

What Should Every Teacher Know About Hearing Impairments?

Moores (1987) notes that

> Although occasional references to education of the deaf may be found, no evidence exists of any organized attempt to provide for the deaf in the United States before the nineteenth century. Parents with the financial resources would send their deaf children to Europe to be educated. (pp. 56–57)

The first permanent school for deaf students in the United States was established by Thomas Hopkins Gallaudet in Connecticut in 1817. The institution was called the American Asylum for the Education and Instruction of the Deaf and Dumb. In 1818, the New York Institution for the Instruction of the Deaf and Dumb was established, and, in 1820, the Pennsylvania Institution for the Deaf and Dumb began. Only four more schools were established in the next 20 years (1820 to 1840), one each in Kentucky, Ohio, Missouri, and Virginia. In the 20 years that followed (1840 to 1860), 20 additional schools were established.

In 1857, the Columbia Institution for the Deaf and Dumb was established in Washington, DC. This school eventually developed a collegiate and later a university unit and is known today as Gallaudet College. It is the only liberal arts university in the world for people who are deaf. In 1869, day classes began in Boston, MA, for students who were deaf. These were the very first special education classes for students with any kind of disability. Today, people with hearing impairments function successfully in general education classrooms and in all walks of life. Most people who are deaf or hard-of-hearing believe that the only barriers to full access and acceptance by society are those erected by the attitudes of people without disabilities. Fortunately, partnerships and collaboration between hearing people and those who are deaf are going a long way toward overcoming these attitudinal obstacles.

DEFINITION

There are two terms used to refer to hearing impairments: deaf and hard-of-hearing. **Deaf** means a hearing loss that prevents a person from understanding speech. People who are deaf have little functional hearing even with a hearing aid; they do not use hearing as their primary sense for gaining information. **Hard-of-hearing** means that a person can process information from sounds and often can benefit from the amplification provided by hearing aids.

The federal definitions of *deaf* and *hard-of-hearing* were enacted with Public Law 94-142 and carried forward with its reauthorizations (Education for All Handicapped Children Act, 1975; Individuals With Disabilities Education Act, 1997; Individuals With Disabilities Education Improvement Act, 2004). They are brief and stress the impact of the impairments on educational performance:

> "Deaf" means having a hearing impairment which is so severe that the child is impaired in processing linguistic information through hearing, with or without amplification, which adversely affects educational performance.
>
> "Hard-of-hearing" means having a hearing impairment, whether permanent or fluctuating, which adversely affects

a child's educational performance but which is not included under the definition of "deaf."

Eligibility for services under the categories of deaf and hard-of-hearing is determined by degree of hearing loss. People with normal hearing can understand speech without a hearing aid. People who are deaf are unable to understand speech, even with the help of a hearing aid. Between normal hearing and deafness are various degrees of hearing loss.

TYPES OF HEARING LOSS

There are two types of hearing loss: conductive and sensorineural. **Conductive hearing loss** is due to blockage or damage to the outer or middle sections of the ear. Conductive losses are generally considered to have less severe effects than sensorineural losses. **Sensorineural hearing loss** occurs when there is damage to the inner ear or auditory nerves.

Some causes of hearing loss are presented in *Table 2.1*. The cause of hearing loss is unknown for about half the people with hearing impairments. Sensorineural hearing losses are caused by viruses like rubella and meningitis for about 14 percent of the people with hearing impairments. Heredity and genetic factors account for about 13 percent of hearing impairments. Knowing the cause of a hearing problem helps teachers and other professionals decide on appropriate treatments. For example, children who are deaf at birth must be taught to communicate differently from children whose hearing loss is acquired after they have learned to talk.

Measuring Hearing

We measure the ability to hear (**auditory acuity**) and hearing loss using two dimensions: intensity and frequency. People hear sounds at specific levels of loudness (intensity). **Loudness** is expressed in decibels (db); the greater the decibel level, the louder the sound. A decibel level of 125 or louder is painful to

Table 2.1 Some Causes of Hearing Impairments

Maternal rubella (5 percent)	Rubella (or German measles) contracted by a pregnant woman may cause hearing loss to the child, depending on when it occurs. It typically results in sensorineural hearing loss.
Meningitis (9 percent)	Meningitis affects the central nervous system and typically results in sensorineural hearing loss.
Otitis media (3 percent)	Otitis media is infection of the middle ear and accumulation of fluid behind the ear drum. Typically it results in conductive hearing loss.
Heredity (13 percent)	There are more than 150 types of genetic deafness.
Other causes at birth (22 percent)	Causes for deafness at birth include high fevers, infections, trauma, birth complications, and prematurity.
Cause unknown (48 percent)	

Source: Moores, D. F. (2001).

the average person. Decibel levels of 0 to 120 are used to test hearing at various frequencies. **Frequency** (or pitch) is measured in hertz (hz), which indicates cycles per second. The frequency range for conversational speech is 500 to 2,000 hz. Both loudness and frequency can be measured with an audiometer.

Hearing loss is described by the lowest decibel level at which a person can hear. Students with slight loss (27–40 db) may have difficulty hearing faint or distant sounds, but will usually not have difficulties in school settings. Students with moderate loss (56–70 db) can usually understand only loud conversations and often experience difficulty using and understanding language. Students with profound loss (91 db or more) may hear loud sounds, but rely more on vision than hearing for communication. Moores (1987) uses characteristics of hearing to define deafness and hardness-of-hearing in terms relative to degrees of hearing loss:

> A "deaf person" is one whose hearing is disabled to an extent (usually 70 db or greater) that precludes the understanding of speech through the ear alone, without or with the use of a hearing aid.
> A "hard-of-hearing person" is one whose hearing is disabled to an extent (usually 35–69 db) that makes difficult, but does not preclude, the understanding of speech through the ear alone, without or with a hearing aid. (p. 9)

Students who are deaf are linked to the world of communication and information primarily through their sight. Most of these students depend on some form of signing to express and receive information. Although most are educated in separate programs, many attend the same classes as their neighbors and peers (U.S. Department of Education, 2001). Typically, students who are hard-of-hearing are enrolled in general education programs and may receive selected special services such as speech and language therapy (Paul & Jackson, 1993).

PREVALENCE

During the 2000–2001 school year, about 71,000 students with hearing impairments received special education services. Since 1990, the proportion of students with hearing impairments who have been served has increased notably, by about 21 percent (U.S. Department of Education, 2002). Students with hearing impairments represent about 0.13 percent of school-age children and adolescents and about 1.2 percent of students with disabilities. There is relatively little variation in the percentage of students identified in each of the states. About 40 percent of students with hearing impairments were served in general education classes for most of the time during the school day (U.S. Department of Education, 2000, 2001, 2002).

Gallaudet University's Research Institute (GRI) has been collecting demographic, audiological, and other educationally relevant information concerning students with impaired hearing since 1968 through its Annual Survey of Deaf and Hard of Hearing Children and Youth. According to GRI's 1999–2000 Regional and National Summary, 55 percent of children in the United States who are deaf were white, 16 percent were black, 21 percent were Hispanic, and 8 percent were of American Indian, Asian/Pacific Islander, multi-ethnic, or other ethnic background (Gallaudet Research Institute, 2001).

WHAT YOU MAY SEE IN YOUR CLASSROOM

In the professional literature, many traits or characteristics are attributed to people who are deaf. Unfortunately, most of them are negative. We say "unfortunately" because the use of negative terminology leads to negative stereotypes about those who are deaf. Moreover, the negative characteristics attributed to people who are deaf generally are not substantiated in empirical studies.

Students with hearing impairments should not be stereotyped. The causes for hearing loss and its effects are simply too varied to lend credence to the concept of a "typical" case. Students with hearing impairments have wide-ranging learning styles and abilities. They do have one characteristic in common: Their ability to hear is limited. This characteristic may be reflected in other cognitive, academic, physical, behavioral, and communication characteristics.

Cognitive Characteristics

There is considerable debate about the extent to which cognitive development is limited by hearing impairments. The environment of people who are deaf or hard-of-hearing is often qualitatively different from that of people who can hear. Much of what we think of as intelligence is developed through hearing and using language. It has been argued that people with hearing impairments do not think in an abstract way and that their intellectual functioning is limited. Moores (1987) puts the theories about the cognitive functioning of students who are deaf into perspective:

> The available evidence suggests that the condition of deafness imposes no limitations on the cognitive capabilities of individuals. There is no evidence to suggest that deaf persons think in more "concrete" ways than the hearing or that their intellectual functioning is in any way less sophisticated. As a group, deaf people function within the normal range of intelligence, and deaf individuals exhibit the same wide variability as the hearing population. ... The great difficulty encountered by deaf children in academic subject matter is most likely not caused by cognitive deficiencies. In fact, it is safe to say that educators of the deaf have not capitalized on the cognitive strengths of deaf children in the academic environment. (pp. 164–165)

Paul and Jackson (1993) believe that differences in cognitive performance between students who are deaf and their hearing peers are more due to the inadequate development of a conventional language system than to limited intellectual ability.

Academic Characteristics

The academic success of a student with a hearing impairment is related to the severity of the hearing loss and the age of the student at its onset as well as the socioeconomic status and hearing status of the student's family. Students who have mild hearing losses generally perform better academically than those with severe losses. Students who are deaf from birth tend to have more difficulty acquiring academic skills than do those who lose their hearing later. Students from families of high socioeconomic status and those who have hearing parents tend to experience fewer academic difficulties than do students from families of low socioeconomic status or those whose parents are hearing impaired.

We cannot make firm generalizations about the ways in which students who are deaf or hard-of-hearing function academically. They do not perform as well as hearing students on standardized tests of reading and writing, and research suggests that children who are deaf have much more difficulty acquiring writing skills than they do acquiring reading skills. But research also suggests that the functional reading ability of students who are deaf is higher than that implied by the scores they earn on standardized achievement tests (Luetke-Stahlman & Luckner, 1991). Clearly, differences in language ability that result from deafness affect a student's ability to perform in traditional academic areas (Paul & Jackson, 1993).

Physical Characteristics

Few physical characteristics are specific to students who are deaf or hard-of-hearing. The widespread belief that the individual compensates for deficiencies in one sense by developing extraordinary abilities in another is unfounded. Students who are deaf or hard-of-hearing have senses of sight, smell, taste, and touch like their peers who do not have hearing impairments.

A characteristic that does differentiate students with hearing impairments from their neighbors and peers is their functional hearing. **Functional hearing** refers to the ability to understand information presented orally and is related to how a student might be taught. For example, a student with a moderate functional hearing loss might not be able to profit from a typical classroom presentation and would require some instructional adaptation to be successful. Most often, functional hearing loss is categorized using decibel groupings (see *Table 2.2*) and related problems.

Behavioral Characteristics

Generalizations about the social, emotional, and behavioral functioning of students who are deaf or hard-of-hearing are based on the performance of these students on standardized tests. But most of these tests are inappropriate for use with this group. Moores (1987) describes two perspectives on the social,

Table 2.2 Characteristics of Functional Hearing Losses

Loss of Function	Hearing Loss (in Decibels)	Symptoms
Normal hearing	Less than 26 db	No significant difficulty with faint speech
Slight	26–40 db	Difficulty only with faint sounds
Mild	41–55 db	Understands face-to-face speech and conversations at 3–5 feet.
Moderate	56–70 db	Frequent difficulty with normal conversation and speech
Severe	71–90 db	Understands only shouted or amplified speech
Profound	91 db or more	Difficulty even with amplified speech

emotional, and behavioral functioning of students who are deaf or hard-of-hearing: one is that students with hearing impairments are deviant and display many problems; the other is that students with hearing impairments are different and need access to services that encourage their optimal development. Based on a review of the research on the social and emotional functioning of people who are deaf, he concludes,

> . . . the evidence suggests that the social-emotional adjustment of the deaf is similar to that of the hearing, with great individual variation. Most deaf individuals cope with the reality of deafness as a life-long condition and lead normal, productive lives. This fact supports the contention that deafness itself has no direct impact, either negative or positive, on the development of a mentally healthy individual. (p. 180)

Deaf Culture

Recent evidence suggests that those who are deaf prefer to be with others who are deaf, that adults who are deaf tend to cluster in groups, socialize, and marry (Moores, 1987, 2001). In other words, people who are deaf experience and design their lives differently from cultural groups of hearing, spoken-language users (Humphries, 1993). They create their own culture, known as **deaf culture**. Accordingly, people who are deaf see the experiences and signed language of their deaf communities as the most important factors in their lives (Anita & Kreimeyer, 2001; Byrnes & Sigafoos, 2001). People who are deaf teach one another how to function in broader society as well as how to get along with others. Sometimes, parents who are deaf want their children to be born deaf, so they can share the culture.

Teachers need to be aware of deaf culture (Byrnes & Sigafoos, 2001; Moores, Jatho, & Creech, 2001). Students who are deaf add to the diversity common in most classrooms. This enhanced diversity may be particularly true in classrooms in which students are deaf and also from ethnic backgrounds:

> It may be more difficult for African-American, Hispanic, Native American, and Asian/Pacific Island students who are deaf to achieve a sense of community in the United States because social forces separate people of different races. Families from ethnic backgrounds may also be isolated from white communities. The forces that isolate children who are deaf from adults who are deaf may be even more pronounced among ethnic groups. There are few "models" of white deaf people in the lives of deaf children, and there are even fewer African-American, Hispanic, Native American, and Asian/Pacific Island deaf role-models in the lives of deaf children. (Humphries, 1993, p. 14)

Integration of People Who Are Deaf

There is considerable debate about the importance of deaf culture and the effect on social development of integrating deaf and hearing students (Moores, Jatho, & Creech, 2001). Most of the research supports integration, but, as with the integration of those with other disabilities, there is a continuing need to focus on critical factors—such as the qualifications, perceptions, attitudes, and demands of teachers as well as the content of the curriculum—within the integrated setting (Paul & Jackson, 1993).

Communication Characteristics

Learning to speak is difficult if you can't hear. Paul and Jackson (1993) argue that "most deaf students have not learned either to speak or sign English at a highly competent level despite the advent and proliferation of signed systems" (pp. 127–128). Largely as a result of this inadequate development of a primary form of English, many students who are deaf experience difficulties in developing the language and literacy skills needed for effective communication.

Communication problems can also interfere with interpersonal relationships. The inability to communicate with other students can delay language development. Students with hearing impairments communicate in ways that are different from those who hear, and this can inhibit their social interaction and development.

Interaction is essential to language development, and much language development and communication skill comes from the interactions between young children and their parents or other caregivers. The hearing families of children who are deaf interact differently with their children than do the hearing families of children who are hard-of-hearing. Children who are deaf are often passive participants in communication, and their parents or caregivers often bombard them with language stimulation and dominate the communication process. Vocabulary and syntax of children who are deaf grow slowly. For teachers, it is useful to know the age of onset of hearing impairments. Children born deaf or with serious hearing impairments are at a significant disadvantage in learning language. Some possible signs of hearing impairments are presented in *Table 2.3;* some general tips for teachers of students with hearing impairments are presented in *Table 2.4.*

Table 2.3   Top Ten Signs of Hearing Impairments

1. Student experiences difficulties following oral presentations and directions.
2. Student watches lips of teachers or other speakers very closely.
3. Student turns head and leans toward speaker.
4. Student uses limited vocabulary.
5. Student uses speech sounds poorly.
6. Student shows delayed language development.
7. Student often does not respond when called from behind.
8. Student is generally inattentive during oral presentations.
9. Student constantly turns volume up on radio or television.
10. Student complains of earaches, has frequent colds or ear infections, or has ear discharge.

Table 2.4   Top Ten Tips for Teachers of Students With Hearing Impairments

1. Reduce the distance between the student and speaker.
2. Reduce background noise as much as possible.
3. Speak slowly and emphasize clear articulation rather than loudness when speaking.
4. Seat the student near the center of desk arrangements.
5. Use face-to-face contact as much as possible.
6. Use complete sentences to provide additional context during conversations or instructional presentations.
7. Use visual cues when referring to objects in the classroom and during instructional presentations.
8. Have classmates take notes during oral presentations for the student to transcribe after the lesson.
9. Encourage independent activities and teach social skills.
10. Make sure the student's hearing aid is turned on and functioning properly.

3

What Should Every Teacher Know About Deafness and Blindness?

S tudents are identified as **deaf-and-blind** or **deaf-blind** when they demonstrate both visual and hearing impairments and when their needs cannot be met in separate programs for students who are deaf or students who are blind (Lieberman & Stuart, 2002). In 1968, the federal government began funding programs for students who are both deaf and blind.

DEFINITION

In 1977, **deaf-blind** was formally defined in federal rules and regulations. The following definition is currently accepted (Individuals With Disabilities Education Act, 1997):

> "Deaf-blind" means concomitant hearing and visual impairments, the combination of which causes such severe communication and other developmental and educational problems that they cannot be accommodated in special

education programs solely for deaf or blind children. (§300.7(c)(2))

The common view of students who are deaf-and-blind is that they are totally deaf and totally blind. This is generally not the case. To be considered deaf-blind, a student must meet the criteria for being considered deaf as well as the criteria for being considered blind. Many students who meet these criteria have some functional hearing and vision.

You probably know the story of Helen Keller, a person who was deaf and blind, who was taught by Anne Sullivan. To put the history of the development of school programs into perspective, you should know that Sullivan began teaching Keller in 1887. Keller received her college degree in 1904. She was the first person who was deaf and blind to do so, some 64 years before the federal government began funding programs for students who are both deaf and blind.

PREVALENCE

During the 2000–2001 school year, about 1,500 students identified as deaf-and-blind received special education services (U.S. Department of Education, 2002). This number is very small (less than 0.01 percent of the school-age population). Although this number has changed little since 1990, it may be far from accurate. We don't have a firm count of students in the deaf-blind category for two reasons: "Parents of such children tend to keep them out of circulation, and . . . once they are located, diagnosis is often ambiguous" (Newland, 1986, p. 577).

Formal identification has increased over the years with the development of **child-find programs** (formal community and public school programs to locate young children with disabilities), but services for students who are deaf-and-blind are still among the least likely to be provided in general education settings. More than 80 percent of these students receiving special education do so in separate classes, separate schools, or in residential facilities (U.S. Department of Education, 2001).

CHARACTERISTICS

The characteristics of students who are deaf-and-blind are a combination of those described for students who are deaf and students who are blind. In addition, these students exhibit more severe academic, social, and communication problems than do students with a single impairment. This is especially evident in communication skills. Students who are blind can benefit from verbal stimulation, and those who are deaf can benefit from visual input. Students who are both blind and deaf rely primarily on other forms of stimulation, such as tactile feedback. Educational programs for these students focus on the use of adapted communication devices and mobility skills.

Bringing Learning to Life: Questions to Ask Parents of Students With Hearing Impairments

Barry's hearing problem was identified early in his life. With the assistance of doctors and other health professionals, his family was able to start special education services during his preschool years. Barry came to school with complete records of his hearing ability and his ability to use speech and language. His teachers were concerned about what Barry could and couldn't do. The school system audiologist and speech-and-language specialist provided answers to the following questions about Barry's educational program:

- What is the range of Barry's hearing in each ear?
- What does Barry's level of hearing loss mean in the classroom?
- How well is Barry using whatever hearing is available?

(Continued)

(Continued)

- How well does Barry understand speech and language constructions?
- How well is Barry using speech in relation to his hearing loss?
- What steps should be followed to help Barry use his available hearing and develop speech and language?

With the answers to these questions, Barry's teachers developed an IEP (individualized education program) to help him achieve continued success and independence.

4

What Tools and Strategies Should Teachers Use to Support Students With Sensory Disabilities?

When the Rehabilitation Act of 1973 and the Education for All Handicapped Children Act of 1975 were passed, I believed wonderful things would happen for people with disabilities. I pictured students with disabilities finally going to school with nondisabled students of the same age and grade, taking the same classes, reading the same books, and taking the same tests. I pictured them participating in the same clubs, sometimes becoming friends and other times not, getting into the same scrapes, and learning how to solve the same problems. I believed that the integrated education that had been atypical for me and other blind students of New Jersey in the 1950s and 1960s would be standard and unremarkable for this generation of disabled students. I assumed that today's high school graduates and college students would have experiences comparable to or better than my own of many years ago. . . . I find that my expectations are only sometimes met. (Asch, 1989, p. 181)

Adrienne Asch's dreams are still only being partially met in U.S. schools, but people all across the country want to improve the lives of students with sensory disabilities, and the students themselves continue to live healthy and productive lives much like those of their neighbors and peers without disabilities. Toward this goal, students with visual and/or hearing impairments can best be helped by teachers who can

Eliminate barriers,

Improve communication, and

Foster independence.

ELIMINATE BARRIERS

When a teacher works with students who are blind, he or she provides an orientation to the classroom (Orr & Rogers, 2002). The teacher points out the location of the teacher's desk, each student's desk, the learning centers, the computer, the pencil sharpener, and all the other places and things the students need to know. Teachers often find it helpful to introduce a few new things each day and to always start students at their own desks as a point of reference for the orientation. Introducing students with vision problems to the classroom environment and school space in a systematic manner helps them to "cognitively map" the physical space and function more effectively in it.

Mobility and information processing (i.e., listening and reading) are key concerns for students who are blind or who have low vision because these students often need assistance accessing their environments. Orientation and mobility training help them develop independence in the environment. Listening-skills training and special methods for reading help students overcome information-accessing problems (see *Table 4.1*).

Technology to Eliminate Barriers

Advances in technology influence how all students are taught. Technology is particularly relevant to students who are

Table 4.1   Interventions to Assist Students With Vision
Impairments

Orientation and Mobility Aids	Orientation is a mental map of our environment. Mobility is the ability to get around in our environment. Guide dogs, canes, and assistance from a sighted person help people make up for orientation and mobility problems caused by vision impairments.
Listening-Skills Training	Many students with vision impairments rely on listening as a primary means of obtaining information. Focusing on a single sound source, analyzing oral information, and focusing on key sound sources are among the listening skills taught to help make up for communication problems caused by vision impairments.
Braille	Some students with vision impairments need to learn to read and write using alternative methods. Braille is a communication system that uses raised dots on paper. People who are blind or who have low vision can read braille text by feeling it. Today, special printers convert computer text files to braille, and paperless braille devices convert information on computer screens to braille output.
Closed-Circuit Television (CCTV)	Many students with vision impairments learn to read using traditional methods with enlarged print. A closed-circuit television system with a small camera and zoom lens, an overhead projector, a microcomputer, and other specialized equipment are used to enlarge text so that it is easier for people with low vision to read.

(Continued)

Table 4.1 (Continued)

Audio Aids	People with visual impairments can hear the information that others can read. Talking books, talking calculators, devices that compress speech to speed it up and eliminate natural pauses, and computer programs that "read" text using scanners all help people with vision impairments make up for their limited sight.
Optical Character Recognition (OCR) Devices	Some students with vision impairments use a computerized scanner (e.g., Kurzweil reader) that converts printed words into synthetic speech. Computer technology has greatly improved OCR. Small sensors can be attached to microcomputers to help people who are blind or those with low vision learn from print.

blind or who have low vision because it helps them access information that sighted people obtain visually (Schrier, Leventhal, & Uslan, 1991). Image enhancing systems, synthetic speech systems, braille technology, and OCR systems, used separately or in combination, provide access to printed information.

Enhanced Image Devices

Improved access to print is provided by **enhanced image** devices. Computer software and hardware or closed-circuit television (CCTV) systems are used to achieve four- to five-times magnification. This magnification helps students with low vision to read text. The most basic computerized systems use word processing software to enlarge text for writing and reading letters, term papers, or other written assignments. More sophisticated systems enlarge everything on the screen, including graphics. A CCTV system uses a video camera to project the magnified image onto a video monitor or television screen. Some of the newer CCTV systems are portable and particularly useful in environments where students need to move around a lot or need information on almost anything within reach, including labels on packages of food and medicine (Uslan, 1993).

Synthetic Speech Devices

Synthetic speech devices are comprised of a synthesizer that does the speaking and a screen access program that tells it what to say. The synthesizer can be a card that is inserted into a computer or an external device that is connected to a computer. The program is loaded into the computer's memory, and the keyboard or keypad is used to input simple commands that tell the synthesizer what to do (e.g., read a word, line, paragraph). Using such a system, the student can access text from an electronic file and have the computer read it aloud. To many people, synthetic speech still implies a robotic quality, but computers increasingly have human-like voices. Talking word processing programs, created to provide auditory feedback to students learning to write, can also assist students with visual impairments. Other talking devices, such as clocks and calculators, are commonplace, and speech output is a feature of more and more products.

Braille Devices

People with visual impairments who read braille use braille display technology, braille printers, and electronic braille notetakers. **Braille display technology** provides access in braille to information on a computer screen. These paperless braille devices, connected to computers, raise or lower a series of pins to produce braille codes for information shown on the computer screen. An advantage of paperless braille displays is that they allow the user to immediately learn the format of the information on the screen; this helps with activities like proofreading (Schrier, Leventhal, & Uslan, 1991).

Braille printers convert information into braille, embossing the braille code onto paper. Braille printers use pins to produce the raised dots formerly done by hand.

Braille note-taking devices are small and portable. Information is entered using a keyboard. A speech synthesizer or braille display provides information. Students with visual impairments use note-taking devices to keep track of information given in classroom presentations or meetings. Sometimes they transfer the information to larger computers to review it or print it on a paperless braille display or traditional printer.

OCR Devices

Optical character recognition (OCR) devices convert print into electronic forms that can be accessed using other adaptive equipment. They work like this: Printed information is scanned using a scanner and converted to electronic text. The text is then accessible using other adaptive devices (e.g., image enhancement, synthetic speech, or braille). Scanners may be hand-held or separate. Some have book-edge options that facilitate the scanning of bound materials. OCR technology is becoming increasingly popular, and costs are decreasing largely because of its widespread use in business (Schrier, Leventhal, & Uslan, 1991). OCR devices that recognize handwriting continue to become more sophisticated and affordable, providing an additional medium for people with visual impairments.

IMPROVE COMMUNICATION

Oral communication is a key concern for students who are deaf or hard-of-hearing (Luckner & Carter, 2001; Luckner & Muir, 2001). Many students with hearing impairments rely on interpreters to help them communicate in educational settings as well as in other situations, such as conferences, workshops, phone calls, and presentations. Interpreters also serve as resources for others interested in interpreting (Luetke-Stahlman & Luckner, 1991). Oral communication, sign systems, total communication, cued speech, finger spelling, assistive listening, and telecommunication devices also help people overcome communication problems caused by hearing impairments (see *Table 4.2*).

Table 4.2   Interventions to Assist Students With Hearing Impairments

Oral Communication	Students with hearing impairments are taught to use speaking and residual hearing as their only means of communicating.
Sign Language	Students with hearing impairments are taught to use manual gestures and body movements as their only means of communicating.
Total Communication	Students with hearing impairments are taught to use oral and sign methods simultaneously as their means of communicating.
Cued Speech	Students with hearing impairments are taught to use visual and manual cues provided by a speaker to decode what is being said.
Assisted Listening Devices	Special types of equipment (including hearing aids, FM transmission and amplification devices, and audio loops) help students with hearing impairments make better use of their residual hearing.
Telecommunication Devices	Closed-captioned television transmissions and teletypewriters connected to telephones take advantage of vision to improve communication for students with hearing impairments. Computer fax/modems and e-mail are now commonplace in this rapidly changing area.

Oral Communication

Oral communication methods emphasize the development and use of skills in the areas of speech, speechreading, and residual hearing. The thrust of this approach is the use of oral English (in English-speaking countries) with all students with hearing impairments. Proponents of this method believe that the goal of education is the development of skills that foster full participation in mainstream (i.e., hearing) society.

Sign Systems

With sign systems, people with hearing impairments express ideas using manual and nonmanual body movements instead of speech (Luckner & Carter, 2001). The **manual** aspects of this form of communication are displayed by shaping, moving, and positioning the hands. **Nonmanual** movements include other parts of the body (e.g., eyes, eyebrows, cheeks, lips, tongue, and shoulders). **American Sign Language (ASL)** is a widely recognized sign language that uses both manual and nonmanual movements. **Finger spelling** is a sign system in which each letter of the alphabet has a finger sign. Using finger spelling, students spell out words used in conversation.

Total Communication

Proponents of total communication methods advocate the use of all modes of communication. In this approach, oral methods and sign systems are used simultaneously. Sign systems that are used prominently within total communication methods share three characteristics (Paul & Jackson, 1993):

They attempt to reproduce the words, parts of words, and word order of English.

They adapt signs from sign language systems.

They develop new signs as they are needed.

Cued Speech

Cued speech involves oral communication and a sign system. In cued speech, eight hand shapes are used in four positions on or near the face to accompany and augment speech. Each hand shape represents a group of consonants or consonant blends and each facial position represents a group of vowel sounds that are used as cues to assist listeners who are speech-reading.

Assistive Listening and Telecommunication

Assistive listening and telecommunication devices take advantage of residual hearing or other senses to enable students to communicate better. **Hearing aids** are the most widely recognized and used assistive listening devices. They are worn in the ear, behind the ear, on the body, or in eyeglass frames. **Classroom amplification systems** are an assistive listening device in which a microphone is used to link the teacher to a student who wears a receiver that often doubles as a hearing aid. When Barry was in preschool, his teacher used a classroom amplification system. Barry's parents thought the system worked pretty well even though Barry didn't need to use it. Some of the students in Barry's class had small receivers attached unobtrusively around their necks. The receivers were connected to a small earplug in one or both ears (depending on the degree of their hearing loss). The teacher talked into a microphone that hung around her neck. When she spoke, she sometimes needed to touch a shoulder or arm to get a student's attention.

Telecommunication devices are small keyboards with screens or printers that can be connected to telephones. Telecommunication devices for the deaf (TDDs), text telephones (TTs), and teletypewriters (TTYs) enable students with hearing impairments to make and receive phone calls. When a call is made, the incoming and outgoing conversation appears on a screen or printer. Fax machines and fax modems also enable students to communicate without speaking or hearing using the phone system at home, school, or work.

Which Method Is Best?

Among the three forms of communication systems (i.e., oral, sign, total), no clear evidence has emerged to support the use of one method over the others (Moores, Jatho, & Creech, 2001; National Association of the Deaf, 2000; Paul & Jackson, 1993). Cued speech is used by a small percentage of students with hearing impairments, mostly from white, upper-middle-class families (Luetke-Stahlman & Luckner, 1991). Assistive listening devices are widely used, and advances in technology have made them smaller, lighter, and more powerful. Telecommunication devices have helped to break down long-standing barriers to communication for people with hearing impairments in employment and social interaction settings.

Foster Independence

Students with sensory disabilities have a wide range of personal and social characteristics that can make them dependent on others. Effective teachers encourage independent activities for these students (Byrnes & Sigafoos, 2001; Orr & Rogers, 2002; Peavey & Leff, 2002). They teach social skills and listening skills as needed, fostering a realistic mix of dependence and independence. They might allow extra time for completion of tasks and use group activities to encourage socialization among general and special education students. Effective teachers learn to use special materials such as manual alphabets, sign language systems, and combined oral and manual communication activities, so they can communicate effectively with students. They work with other teachers who have suggestions for alternative classroom activities, materials, and instructional units. Effective teachers are aware of the delicate balance that exists between needing special assistance and wanting to be "normal." They are concerned with the impressions a student's special learning needs create, and they try to minimize the extent to which a student is treated negatively because of them.

A goal of teaching is fostering independence. Effective teachers consider how students' special needs may affect learning and adjust their instruction accordingly. To work more effectively and foster the independence of students with visual and hearing impairments, try the following tactics:

When presenting print materials and pictures on chalkboards, overhead projectors, and other visual media, verbalize the text and describe the pictures.

When using videotapes, movies, and slides, narrate non-verbal actions or scenes.

Seat students with vision problems with their backs to windows or other sources of light to avoid glare on instructional materials.

Seat students near the chalkboard or other places where demonstrations are given, or give them the freedom to move closer to areas of instruction.

Create contrast with dark-lined paper and soft pencils (or felt-tip pens), helping students with vision problems to better discern information. Word processors and typewriters also can be useful in creating contrast.

Seat students with hearing problems near your desk and at the center of desk arrangements.

Use face-to-face contact as much as possible. Don't turn away from students with hearing impairments during a conversation or instructional lesson.

Use complete sentences when talking to students with hearing problems because they provide more context for understanding a conversation.

Use visual cues for students with hearing problems when referring to objects in the room and during instructional units (such as the outline of a lesson written on the board or a handout).

Have a student take notes for a child with a hearing impairment; then have the student transcribe the notes after the oral presentation.

Arrange seating so that distracting noises are kept to a minimum for students with hearing aids.

Bringing Learning to Life:
Tips for Interacting Positively With
Students Who Have Sensory Disabilities

Ever take a different path to avoid a person who is blind? Ever raise your voice when speaking to a person who is blind? Ever stare at people using sign language? Don't worry about it; most people have, largely because they have limited experience with people with sensory disabilities. Here are some tips for interacting positively with people with vision and hearing impairments.

- Speak first. Remember that you have the advantage in social and instructional situations. You can see the student and the environment. You can hear the student and the environmental sounds. Let students with sensory disabilities know you are there and happy to see them.
- Use natural language. Don't be afraid to say "see" or "look" around a student with a vision impairment. Use the student's name when speaking. Use a natural tone of voice and volume unless the student requests you to change either.
- If the student indicates that he or she doesn't understand what you are saying, rephrase the message and repeat it; be careful not to simply say the same words louder.
- Be precise when giving directions or describing things.
- Allow time for students to complete simple tasks. Planning ahead fosters independence. Doing the task for a student because you want it done quickly doesn't foster independence.
- Use outlines as guides and use overhead projectors to avoid turning away from the class during oral presentations.

- During group discussions, have one student speak at a time and use the name of the speaker to facilitate communication and understanding.
- Give students with hearing or vision impairments the benefit of the doubt when making decisions about disabilities. Don't assume problems exist just because a student doesn't see or hear as well as others.

5

Sensory Disabilities in Perspective

Sensory impairments can have serious educational implications. Students who are blind and/or deaf have unique educational needs that can be accommodated in general education classes with the assistance of other professionals, material and environmental modifications, and disability-specific curriculum content. Often, the biggest obstacle to success, in any environment, is the negative attitudes of teachers, neighbors, coworkers, and friends toward the capabilities of students with sensory disabilities. According to Dr. I. King Jordan, the first president of Gallaudet University (who is deaf), an attitude that is making a difference today is that "[d]eaf people can do anything hearing people can do . . . except hear!" (as cited in Singleton, 1992). His words speak broadly for a movement toward empowerment in which people who are deaf are taking control of their lives and demanding active roles in the decision making that affects them.

This "empowerment movement" has its seeds in the civil rights movement of the 1960s, the women's movement of the 1970s, and the technological revolution of the 1980s (which opened new avenues of communication for people with hearing impairments). The empowerment movement has broad implications for all people with disabilities. The following suggestions for empowering students who are deaf are relevant for other groups as well (Singleton, 1992):

Encourage research on deaf history and the development of deaf studies programs to provide the deaf community a means of sharing their cultural identity with each other, their families, the community, and the world.

Foster pride in being deaf and encourage Deaf Awareness Day or Deaf Awareness Week activities.

Recognize the deaf community as having a unique identity and a unique language: ASL (American Sign Language).

Teach respect for differences among individuals.

Place qualified people who are deaf in important leadership roles in programs and organizations for deaf people.

Maintain a majority of deaf and hard-of-hearing persons as representatives on decision-making boards for programs affecting deaf people.

Enforce all provisions of the Americans With Disabilities Act (1990) to provide deaf, deaf-blind, and hard-of-hearing people with full access to society.

Provide opportunities for socialization with other children or adults who are deaf.

Educate parents about deafness and sign language so they can provide full communication to their children from birth.

Increase the numbers of qualified deaf and hard-of-hearing teachers, counselors, and administrators in educational programs as positive role models.

Require certified educational interpreters in mainstreamed programs.

Provide full access to educational programs and employment training opportunities.

Provide a tax deduction for the purchase of assistive listening devices such as Text Telephones and Braille TDDs.

Include placement in residential schools as an option for students who are deaf.

Require individualized education programs (IEPs) tailored to the student's individual needs after appropriate evaluations have been done by professionals trained in deafness. (p. 13)

UNDERSTAND CHARACTERISTICS

There are few characteristics specific to the special education categories of learning disabilities, speech and language impairments, mental retardation, and emotional disturbance. Few educational interventions are specific to these categories; therefore implications for education need to be drawn from the behaviors of individual students rather than from the categories. Things are different with sensory disabilities. Some characteristics are specific to sensory disabilities. These characteristics affect functioning and have specific educational implications. People with visual or hearing impairments process sensory information in unique ways. Knowing that a student is blind or has low vision, or is deaf or hard-of-hearing, provides useful and important information for planning instruction for that student.

SUPPORT ACCOMMODATIONS

The kinds of accommodations teachers and schools must make for students who demonstrate sensory disabilities are a function of the specific nature of each student's visual or auditory impairment. Many students with sensory disabilities function with very few modifications in their lives, and the implications of living with a sensory disability can be minimal. Some modifications simply make sense. For example, when teachers see that lighting is inadequate for students with low vision, they provide additional lighting. Sometimes teachers provide access to print materials through magnification or provide special writing materials, such as wide-lined paper and felt-tip pens, to help students complete assignments. When working with students who are deaf, teachers learn manual communication systems to help convey and obtain information. They learn how to identify and correct problems with assistive listening devices and other aids. They also arrange classroom seating to reduce distractions, helping students with sensory disabilities focus and obtain information from instructional presentations. While many of these interventions may help other students as well, they are not considered necessary or essential for them to be successful in school.

Bringing Learning to Life: Basic Troubleshooting for Hearing Aids

Like many students with hearing impairments, Barry came to school with an assistive listening device. At first, his teacher worried about what she would do if the hearing aid failed. She figured that making sure the equipment was working was one of the most important things she would do during the day and decided it was her responsibility to be knowledgeable about the equipment that her students were using. She contacted some people, and they provided the "troubleshooting guide for people with hearing aids" shown in Table 5.1, based on information presented in Barbara Luetke-Stahlman and John Luckner's (1991) book.

The specialists also suggest a classroom kit for general hearing-aid maintenance that contains the following:

1. Battery tester

2. Replacement batteries

3. Pipe cleaners and/or cotton swabs

4. Forced-air spray cleaner

5. Toothpicks and a set of tweezers

6. Small cleaning brush or toothbrush

7. Small roll of tape

The specialists encouraged the teacher to contact Barry's parents for additional ideas and to work closely with them if she spotted any problems with the hearing aid that required professional care or maintenance. While Barry was in her room, the teacher didn't have any problems with his assistive listening device, but she passed on what she knew to his next teacher.

Table 5.1 Troubleshooting Guide for People With Hearing Aids

Symptom	Possible Problem	Possible Solution
Hearing aid not working or not working well	Dead batteries	Check batteries, or try new ones
	Batteries not properly placed	
	Earmold plugged with water or wax	Disconnect earmold, rinse with warm water, dry and/or clear with pipe cleaner or cotton swab
Hearing aid whistles or gives distracting feedback	Punctured or kinked tubing	Replace or straighten tubing
	Earmold not properly fitted in the ear	Insert earmold properly
	Earmold plugged with water or wax	Disconnect earmold, rinse with warm water, dry and/or clear with pipe cleaner or cotton swab
	Receiver close to wall or other reflecting surface	Reposition student
Poor tone quality or distortion	Punctured or cracked tubing	Replace or straighten tubing
	Earmold not properly fitted in ear	Insert earmold properly
	Earmold plugged with water or wax	Disconnect earmold, rinse with warm water, dry and/or clear with pipe cleaner or cotton swab
	Receiver close to wall or other reflecting surface	Reposition student
	Microphone clogged	Clean microphone

Foster Collaboration

Classroom teachers of students with sensory disabilities also work closely with professionals serving in itinerant and consultative roles. Often, but not always, this means teachers are expected to communicate effectively and coordinate programs jointly with families, paraprofessionals, specialists, administrators, and other professionals. Cooperative relations are essential when identifying the strengths and weaknesses of students with sensory disabilities and when setting instructional objectives for these students. Itinerant teachers and consultants often help teachers understand the impact of vision or hearing loss on academic and social development. They help teachers learn more about the uses of assistive technology (e.g., hearing aids, interpreters, and braille technology). The key to successful collaboration is ongoing communication and up-to-date information.

Itinerant teachers work with local educational teams and provide disability-specific instruction to students with sensory disabilities, such as braille reading and writing and sign language. The itinerant specialist is a key player in ensuring that the educational needs of students are met. It is crucial to involve the itinerant specialist in all phases of implementing a student's education, including assessment, IEP team meetings, and delivery of instructional services.

Prepare for the Future

Positive attitudes toward including students with sensory disabilities in classrooms with their neighbors and peers have improved their lives. Major technological advances have also changed the ways in which and the extent to which these students participate in and benefit from schooling. The future is bright. Over the next ten years, new technologies will enable larger numbers of students to participate more fully in educational programs.

6

What Have We Learned?

As you complete your study of teaching students with sensory disabilities, it may be helpful to review what you have learned. To help you check your understanding of teaching students with sensory disabilities, we have listed the key points and key vocabulary for you to review. We have included the Self-Assessment again, so you can compare what you know now with what you knew as you began your study. Finally, we provide a few topics for you to think about and some activities for you to do "on your own."

KEY POINTS

▣ Students with sensory disabilities have impairments that affect how well they see and/or hear. Overall, about 2 percent of students with disabilities have vision or hearing impairments (U.S. Department of Education, 2001).

▣ Vision impairments include blindness and low vision.

▣ Blindness and low vision are measured by acuity and field of vision.

▣ Students with hearing impairments are referred to as deaf or hard-of-hearing.

53

▣ Hearing impairments are measured in units of loudness (decibels) and frequency (hertz).

▣ The cause of hearing impairment is unknown for about half the cases. Rubella, meningitis, otitis media, and genetic transmission are the main known causes.

▣ Often, the greatest obstacle to success for people with sensory disabilities is the attitude of people who go to school, live, and work with them.

▣ Students are categorized as deaf-and-blind when they demonstrate both visual and hearing impairments and when their needs cannot be met in separate programs for students with visual or hearing impairments alone.

▣ Students with sensory disabilities have specific educational needs. Needs associated with vision impairments relate to information and environmental access. Needs associated with hearing impairments relate to the learning and use of language.

▣ With the exception of their problems hearing or seeing, students with sensory disabilities learn much like other students. With the aid of rapidly developing technology, they are participating more fully in general education classrooms with their neighbors and peers.

More About Visual Impairments

Prevalence

The number of children born with visual impairments is about 12 per 1,000. Severe visual impairments (legally or totally blind) occur at a rate of .06 per 1,000.

Characteristics

The effect of visual problems on a child's development depends on the severity, type of loss, age at which the condition appears, and the child's overall functioning level. Many children who have multiple disabilities may also have visual impairments resulting in motor, cognitive, or social developmental delays.

A young child with visual impairments has little reason to explore interesting objects in the environment and thus may miss opportunities to have experiences and to learn. This lack of exploration may continue until learning becomes motivating or until intervention begins.

Because the child cannot see parents or peers, he or she may be unable to imitate social behavior or understand nonverbal cues. Visual disabilities can create obstacles to a growing child's independence.

Educational Implications

Children with visual impairments should be assessed early to benefit from early intervention programs. Technology in the form of computers and low-vision optical and video aids enables many children who are partially sighted, have low vision, or are blind to participate in general education class activities. Large-print materials, books on tape, and braille books are available.

Students with visual impairments may need additional help with special equipment and modifications in the general education curriculum to emphasize listening skills, communication, orientation and mobility, vocation and career options, and daily living skills. Students with low vision or those who are legally blind may need help to use their residual vision more efficiently and to work with special aids and materials. Students who have visual impairments combined with other types of disabilities have a greater need for an interdisciplinary approach and may require greater emphasis on self-care and daily living skills.

Source: Used with the permission of the National Dissemination Center for Children with Disabilities (NICHCY).

More About Hearing Impairments

Prevalence

Hearing loss and deafness affect individuals of all ages and may occur at any time from infancy through old age. The U.S. Department of Education (2002) reports that, during the 2000–2001 school year, 70,767 students aged 6 to 21 (or 1.2 percent of all students with disabilities) received special education services under the category of hearing impairment. However, the number of children with hearing loss and deafness is undoubtedly higher, since many of these students may have other disabilities as well and may be served under other categories.

Characteristics

It is useful to know that sound is measured by its loudness or intensity (measured in units called decibels, db) and its frequency or pitch (measured in units called hertz, hz). Impairments in hearing can occur in either or both areas, and may exist in only one ear or in both ears. Hearing loss is generally described as slight, mild, moderate, severe, or profound, depending upon how well a person can hear the intensities or frequencies most greatly associated with speech. Generally, only children whose hearing loss is greater than 90 decibels (db) are considered deaf for the purposes of educational placement.

There are four types of hearing loss. **Conductive hearing losses** are caused by diseases or obstructions in the outer or middle ear (the conduction pathways for sound to reach the inner ear). Conductive hearing losses usually affect all frequencies of hearing evenly and do not result in severe losses. A person with a conductive hearing loss usually is able to use a hearing aid well or can be helped medically or surgically.

Sensorineural hearing losses result from damage to the delicate sensory hair cells of the inner ear or the nerves which supply it. These hearing losses can range from mild to profound. They often affect the person's ability to hear certain frequencies more than others. Thus, even with amplification to increase the sound level, a person with a sensorineural hearing loss may perceive distorted sounds, sometimes making the successful use of a hearing aid impossible.

Mixed hearing losses are a combination of conductive and sensorineural losses. This means that a problem occurs in both the outer or middle ear and the inner ear. **Central hearing losses** result from damage or impairment to the nerves or nuclei of the central nervous system, either in the pathways to the brain or in the brain itself.

Educational Implications

Hearing loss or deafness does not affect a person's intellectual capacity or ability to learn. However, children who are either hard-of-hearing or deaf generally require some form of special education services in order to receive an adequate education. Such services may include

Regular speech, language, and auditory training from a specialist

Amplification systems

Services of an interpreter for those students who use manual communication

Favorable seating in the class to facilitate speechreading

Captioned films and videos

Assistance of a note-taker, who takes notes for the student with a hearing loss, so that the student can fully attend to instruction

Instruction for the teacher and peers in alternate communication methods, such as sign language; and counseling.

Children who are hard-of-hearing will find it much more difficult than children who have normal hearing to

(Continued)

(Continued)

learn vocabulary, grammar, word order, idiomatic expressions, and other aspects of verbal communication. For children who are deaf or have severe hearing losses, early, consistent, and conscious use of visible communication modes (such as sign language, finger spelling, and cued speech), amplification, and aural/oral training can help reduce this language delay. By age 4 or 5, most children who are deaf are enrolled in school on a full-day basis and do special work on communication and language development. It is important for teachers and audiologists to work together to teach these children to use their residual hearing to the maximum extent possible, even if the preferred means of communication is manual. Since the great majority of deaf children (over 90 percent) are born to hearing parents, programs should provide instruction for parents on the implications of deafness within the family.

People with hearing loss use oral or manual means of communication or a combination of the two. Oral communication includes speech, speechreading, and the use of residual hearing. Manual communication involves signing and finger spelling. Total communication, as a method of instruction, is a combination of the oral method plus signing and finger spelling.

Individuals with hearing loss, including those who are deaf, now have many helpful devices available to them. Text telephones (TTs), teletypewriters (TTYs), and telecommunications devices for the deaf (TDDs) enable persons to type phone messages over the telephone network. The telecommunications relay service (TRS), now required by law, makes it possible for TT users to communicate with virtually anyone (and vice versa) via telephone. The National Institute on Deafness and Other Communication Disorders Information Clearinghouse (800) 241-1044 (voice) or (800) 241-1055 (TT) makes available lists of TRS numbers by state.

Source: Used with the permission of the National Dissemination Center for Children with Disabilities (NICHCY).

KEY VOCABULARY

American Sign Language (ASL) is a widely recognized sign language that uses both manual and nonmanual movements.

Astigmatism is a condition in which the eyes produce images that are not equally in focus.

Auditory acuity is a measurement of the ability to hear using two indicators: intensity and frequency.

Blindness is central visual acuity of 20/200 or less in the better eye with correction or central visual acuity of more than 20/200 if there is a visual field defect in which the peripheral field is contracted to such an extent that the widest diameter of the visual field subtends an angular distance no greater than 20 degrees in the better eye.

Braille display technology provides access in braille to information on a computer screen.

Braille printers convert information into braille, embossing the braille code onto paper.

Child-find programs are formal community and public school programs to locate young children with disabilities.

Conductive hearing loss is due to blockage or damage to the outer or middle sections of the ear.

Deaf-and-blind or **deaf-blind** refers to the sensory impairments of individuals who demonstrate both visual and hearing impairments and whose needs cannot be met in separate programs for students who are deaf or students who are blind.

Deaf culture refers to a unique view of life or culture created by people who are deaf and who consequently experience and design their lives differently from cultural groups of hearing, spoken-language users.

Deafness is a condition in which a person's hearing loss prevents the understanding of speech. People who are deaf have little functional hearing even with a hearing aid; they do not use hearing as their primary sense for gaining information.

Deafness and blindness is the phrase used to refer to a combination of hearing and visual impairments.

Enhanced image devices are either computer software and hardware systems or closed-circuit television (CCTV) systems that are used to achieve magnification.

Finger spelling is a sign system in which each letter of the alphabet has a finger sign.

Frequency (pitch) is measured in hertz (hz), in other words, cycles per second.

Functional hearing refers to the ability to understand information presented orally and is related to how a student might be taught.

Hard-of-hearing is a condition in which a person can process information from sounds and often can benefit from the amplification provided by hearing aids.

Hearing impairment refers to a deficiency in hearing, whether permanent or fluctuating, that adversely affects one's educational performance or employment.

Hyperopia (farsightedness) is a condition in which people see objects at a distance but not those that are close.

Legally blind means a person needs to stand at a distance of 20 feet to see what a person with normal vision can see from 200 feet away.

Loudness is expressed in decibels (db); the greater the decibel level, the louder the sound.

Low vision describes a severe visual impairment that is not necessarily limited to distance vision. Individuals who have some sight but are unable to read newsprint at a normal viewing distance, even with the aid of eyeglasses or contact lenses, are considered to have low vision. These individuals use a combination of vision and other senses to learn, and they generally require adaptations in lighting, the size of print, or braille.

Manual movements are displayed by shaping, moving, and positioning the hands.

Mobility is the ability to move safely and efficiently from one place to another.

Myopia (nearsightedness) is a condition in which people see objects that are close but not those at a distance.

Nonmanual movements are made by parts of the body other than the hands (e.g., eyes, eyebrows, cheeks, lips, tongue, and shoulders).

Normal field of vision means being able to see objects within a range of approximately 180 degrees.

Nystagmus is a rapid, involuntary lateral, vertical, or rotary movement of the eye that interferes with bringing objects into focus.

Ocular motility problems affect the eyes' ability to move smoothly and focus properly.

Optical character recognition (OCR) devices convert print into electronic forms that can be accessed using other adaptive equipment.

Orientation refers to the ability to know where one is in relation to the environment.

Partially sighted refers to a visual problem that has resulted in a need for special education services.

Sensorineural hearing loss occurs when there is damage to the inner ear or auditory nerves.

Strabismus describes an inability to focus both eyes on the same object, causing one eye to become nonfunctional and vision to be affected.

Synthetic speech devices are comprised of a synthesizer that does the speaking and a screen access program that tells it what to say.

Visual acuity is the ability to see things at specified distances.

Visual impairment refers to a functional loss of vision that, even with correction, adversely affects a child's educational performance.

Visual impairments can refer to all degrees of vision loss.

Self-Assessment 2

After you complete this book, check your knowledge and understanding of the content covered. Choose the best answer for each of the following questions.

1. The term that refers to all degrees of vision loss is

    a. visual impairments

    b. blind

    c. legally blind

    d. deaf and blind

2. A _____ problem may make it difficult to see things clearly in the central visual field but relatively easy in the peripheral field.

    a. field of vision

    b. low vision

    c. visual acuity

    d. visual directive

3. Myopia, a term that describes the phenomenon of distant objects being blurry while close objects are in focus, is commonly called

    a. ocular motility

    b. nearsightedness

    c. astigmatism

    d. strabismus

4. Problems that affect the eyes' ability to move smoothly and focus properly refer to

   a. ocular motility

   b. farsightedness

   c. astigmatism

   d. nystagmus

5. During the past ten years, the number of students provided special education services for visual impairments has

   a. increased

   b. remained constant

   c. decreased

   d. decreased and then increased

6. The term that refers to all degrees of hearing loss is

   a. sensory disorders

   b. deaf

   c. hard-of-hearing

   d. hearing impairments

7. Hearing loss that prevents understanding of speech through the ear, with or without a hearing aid, is called

   a. hard-of-hearing

   b. deafness

   c. deaf and blind

   d. mild hearing loss

8. Auditory acuity is measured through

   a. intensity and frequency

   b. intensity and hertz

   c. frequency and decibels

   d. decibels and intensity

9. Loudness is measured in

   a. sound waves

   b. decibels

   c. hertz

   d. avis

10. A widely recognized sign language that uses both manual and other movements is called

    a. Original Sign Language

    b. Cued Speech

    c. Manual Speech and Language

    d. American Sign Language

REFLECTION

After you answer the multiple-choice questions, think about how you would answer the following questions:

- What factors might affect the academic success of individuals with visual impairments?
- What factors might affect the academic success of individuals with hearing impairments?
- What do effective teachers do to provide support for students with visual and hearing impairments?

Answer Key for Self-Assessments

1.   a

2.   a

3.   b

4.   a

5.   c

6.   d

7.   b

8.   a

9.   b

10.   d

On Your Own

☑ Draw a diagram illustrating how the following words or phrases are related to each other: auditory acuity, conductive, deaf, decibel, frequency, hard-of-hearing, hearing loss, hertz, intensity, and sensorineural. Write a short paragraph that describes the diagram.

☑ Prepare a two- or three-page outline for a presentation to elementary school students on deafness. Answer the following questions as part of the presentation:

What does it mean to be deaf?

What do people with deafness or hearing impairments hear?

What causes deafness?

Are people who are deaf able to speak?

If someone is born deaf, how does he or she learn to speak?

Do people with hearing impairments hear better at some times than at others?

Can people who are deaf use the phone and watch television?

☑ Contact the American Foundation for the Blind (see Resources) or a similar local, state, or national organization that focuses on people with sensory disabilities. Ask for information on the purpose of the organization, its membership, and its services. Ask for information describing how technology is being used to improve services provided to people with sensory disabilities.

☑ Browse through a journal or textbook that focuses on students with sensory disabilities. Review the table of contents. Note the information and articles that are included (e.g., research, opinion, practical suggestions). Check the references provided. Find at least three articles that describe specific teaching activities that you could use to help students with visual impairments be successful in your classroom. Find at least three articles that describe specific teaching activities that you could use to help students with hearing impairments be successful in your classroom.

☑ To better understand how people with sensory disabilities experience the world, try some of these simulations, and note your reactions to them:

Blindfold yourself, and get ready for work as you would on any other day.

Blindfold yourself, and have a friend take you on a tour.

Go to the middle of a park with a friend, blindfold yourself, and find your way home with your friend acting as a guide.

Watch television for one hour with the sound turned off.

Watch television for one hour with the sound very low.

Have a conversation with a friend using only gestures.

☑ Research how many television programs are accessible to people with hearing impairments. For three days, look for evidence of closed-captioning during television programs or in a TV guide. Prepare a graph illustrating the types of shows that are available (e.g., drama, comedy, news, movies).

☑ Find out what it is like to have a frequency hearing loss. Write four sentences of 8 to 10 words each. Write them again leaving out the following letters and letter combinations: s, sh, ch, t, th, p, and f. Try to figure out the words by reading them. Read the rewritten sentences to a couple of friends and have them figure them out. Try these sentences if you can't think of any:

Those shells are cheap, but I still don't want them.

Please put the food on the small shelf.

Children, please wait before charging across the street!

It takes two people to communicate, even if only one can hear.

She sells seashells at the seashore.

☑ Volunteer to work in a setting where people with sensory disabilities are provided services. Participate for at least two hours on five occasions. Describe the jobs you were given. Describe assistance you were provided by professionals. Describe how you would organize a volunteer experience if you were working in the same setting.

☑ Provide child care for a family with a child with a hearing impairment for a total of six hours on several different days. Prepare a childcare guide with things to remember when spending time with children with hearing impairments.

☑ Find a telephone with a TDD and make a call to the Council for Exceptional Children (see Resources). Request information about divisions within the organization that provide services to people interested in students with sensory disabilities. The phone number is (703) 620-3660; tell the receptionist you want to use the TDD phone.

Resources

WEB SITES

American Foundation for the Blind (AFB). Search the AFB's service center on the Web to identify services for blind and visually impaired persons in the United States and Canada: www.afb .org/services.asp.

BOOKS

Bergman, T. (1989). *Finding a common language: Children living with deafness.* Milwaukee, WI: Gareth Stevens. In a book suitable for young readers and filled with photographs powerfully illustrating children's personalities and moods, Bergman shows that a disability should not be a cause for embarrassment, separation, or fear.

Branson, J., & Miller, D. (2001). *Damned for their difference: The cultural construction of deaf people as disabled.* Washington, DC: Gallaudet University Press. Until the recent recognition of deaf culture and the legitimacy of signed languages, societies around the world have classified people who are deaf as "disabled," a term that separates all persons so designated from the mainstream in a disparaging way. This book offers a well-founded explanation of how this discrimination came to be.

Cassie, D. (1984). *So who's perfect! People with visible differences tell their own stories.* Scottdale, PA: Herald Press. Cassie provides an excellent compilation of the experiences of people with disabilities, including those who are deaf, hard-of-hearing, blind, and partially sighted.

Christensen, K. M., & Delgado, G. L. (Eds.). (1993). *Multicultural issues in deafness.* White Plains, NY: Longman. Deaf culture and populations of children and youth who are deaf are discussed.

Christian, M. B. (1986). *Mystery at Camp Triumph.* Morton Grove, IL: Whitman. After being blinded in an accident, Angie resents going to a camp for people with disabilities. She becomes involved in a mystery and develops confidence and independence as a result. This is an excellent book for upper elementary students.

Cohen, I. H. (1994). *Train go sorry: Inside a school for the deaf.* Boston, MA: Houghton Mifflin. As a child, Leah put pebbles in her ears as make-believe hearing aids. She was raised on the grounds of the Lexington School for the Deaf where her father is superintendent. In *"Train Go Sorry,"* she describes her experiences and provides valuable insight into issues raised in the deaf culture movement.

Greenberg, J. E. (1985). *What is the sign for friend?* New York: Franklin Watts. This children's book includes common manual signs (e.g., deaf, school, friend). Even though Shane is born deaf, he can do almost anything his hearing friends can.

Holbrook, M. C. (Ed.). (1996). *Children with visual impairments: A parents' guide.* Bethesda, MD: Woodbine. (800) 843-7323 or (301) 897-3570. www.woodbinehouse.com.

Lewis, S., & Allman, C. B. (2000). Seeing eye to eye: An administrator's guide to students with low vision. New York: American Foundation for the Blind. (800) 232-3044. www.afb.org.

Luetke-Stahlman, B., & Luckner, J. (1991). *Effectively educating students with hearing impairments.* White Plains, NY: Longman.

This excellent resource illustrates key factors related to planning for and delivering instruction to students with hearing impairments. The chapter on "working with others" is particularly useful.

Luterman, D. M. (1991). *When your child is deaf: A guide for parents.* Parkton, MD: York Press. (800) 962-2763. *www.yorkpress .com/index.html.*

Medwid, D. J., & Weston, D. C. (1995). *Kid-friendly parenting with deaf and hard-of-hearing children: A treasury of fun activities toward better behavior.* Washington, DC: Gallaudet University Press. (800) 621-2736; (888) 630-9347 (Voice/TTY). *http:// gupress.gallaudet.edu.*

Moores, D. F. (2001). *Educating the deaf: Psychology, principles, and practices* (5th ed.). Boston: Houghton Mifflin. This comprehensive overview addresses key concepts related to definition, identification, causes, and treatments. It is widely used and accepted as an introductory text on deafness and hearing impairments.

Moores, D. F., & Meadow-Orlans, K. P. (Eds.). (1990). *Educational and developmental aspects of deafness.* Washington, DC: Gallaudet University Press. The text includes school and home aspects of deafness; a comparison of students from Israel, Denmark, and the United States who are deaf; and responses to hearing loss in later life.

Ogden, P. W. (1996). *The silent garden: Raising your deaf child* (Rev. ed.). Washington, DC: Gallaudet University Press. (800) 621-2736; (888) 630-9347 (Voice/TTY). *http://gupress.gallaudet. edu.*

Paul, P. V., & Jackson, D. W. (1993). *Toward a psychology of deafness: Theoretical and empirical perspectives.* Boston: Allyn & Bacon. This is a comprehensive overview of the impact of deafness on important aspects of cognitive, psychological, and social development. It focuses on individuals with severe hearing loss.

Rezen, S. V., & Hausman, C. (1985). *Coping with hearing loss. A guide for adults and their families.* New York: Dembner Books.

This provides a sensitive treatment of the physical and psychological effects of hearing loss and how people cope with and overcome hearing problems.

Sardegna, J., Shelly, S., Shelly, A., & Steidl, S. M. (2002). *The encyclopedia of blindness and vision impairment* (2nd ed.). New York: Facts on File. More than 500 detailed entries with a minimum of technical jargon provide a history of blindness and vision impairment with an A-to-Z presentation of health issues, types of surgery, medications, medical terminology, social issues, myths and misconceptions, economic issues, and current research trends. It also provides statistics on blindness and vision impairment, information on schools for the blind, and relevant Web sites for further study.

Scholl, G. (Ed.). (1986). *Foundations of education for blind and visually handicapped children and youth.* New York: American Foundation for the Blind. This edited text addresses key areas related to sensory disabilities involving vision.

Schwartz, S. (1987). *Choices in deafness: A parent's guide.* Kensington, MD: Woodbine House. Trends in educating people with hearing impairments as well as an overview and description of cued speech, oral communication, and total communication approaches are presented. This is an excellent resource for parents and teachers.

Scott, E., Jan, J., & Freeman, R. (1995). *Can't your child see?* (2nd ed.). Austin, TX: Pro-Ed. (512) 451-3246. www.proedinc.com.

Smith, E. S. (1987). *A guide dog goes to school: The story of a dog trained to lead the blind.* New York: William Morrow. In this book for young readers, Cinderella is transformed from a frisky, friendly puppy into a loving and responsible companion. She capably leads her master who is blind along crowded streets and through bustling crowds.

Tucker, B. P. (1997). *Idea advocacy for children who are deaf or hard-of-hearing: A question and answer book for parents and professionals.* San Diego, CA: Singular. (800) 521-8545. www.singpub.com.

Turkington, C., & Sussman, A. E. (2001). *Encyclopedia of deafness and hearing disorders* (2nd ed.). New York: Facts on File. This comprehensive reference offers basic information on deafness and hearing disorders, from types of conditions to the legal rights of those with hearing impairments, treatment options, and degrees of hearing loss.

Walker, I. A. (1985). *Amy: The story of a deaf child.* New York: E. P. Dutton. In her own words, Amy talks about her life with her friends and family, at school and at home. With more than 100 photographs, this is a wonderful portrait of a girl whose parents went to court because they wanted her to have the same opportunities as her peers. It includes photos showing Amy signing common words.

Warren, D. (1984). *Blindness and early childhood development.* New York: American Foundation for the Blind. This excellent resource discusses the effects of blindness on infancy, early childhood, perception, intelligence, and cognitive abilities.

Journals and Articles

American Annals of the Deaf (AAD). Donald Moores, Editor, *AAD*, 409 Fowler Hall, 800 Florida Avenue N.E., Washington, DC 20002. *AAD* is a professional journal dedicated to quality education and related services for children and adults who are deaf or hard-of-hearing. It serves as a primary source of information and research on education, deafness, and related topics. Subscribers also receive the *Annual Reference Issue,* a comprehensive, detailed guide compiled by Gallaudet University researchers that lists schools and programs in the United States and Canada for people who are deaf and hard-of-hearing.

Case, B. A. (2000). Using analogy to develop an understanding of deaf culture. A K–5 curriculum. *Multicultural Education, 7*(3), 41–44. This model for a multicultural curriculum introduces aspects of deaf culture to hearing students. Deaf culture is explained, and analogy and empathy are presented as catalysts for change in multicultural settings.

Journal of Speech, Language, and Hearing Research (JSLHR). American Speech-Language-Hearing Association, 10801 Rockville Pike, Rockville, MD 20852. Published by the American Speech-Language-Hearing Association, *JSLHR* pertains broadly to studies of the process and disorders of speech, hearing, and language. Experimental reports; theoretical, tutorial, or review papers; brief research notes describing clinical procedures or instruments; and letters to the editor are published.

Journal of Visual Impairment & Blindness (JVIB). Alan Koenig, Editor in Chief, JVIB, College of Education, Texas Tech University, Box 41071, Lubbock, TX 79409. Published by the American Foundation for the Blind and now a two-part bimonthly publication, *JVIB* is *the* research publication, an international, interdisciplinary journal of record on blindness and visual impairment. *JVIB News Service* is a newsletter digest of information and innovative ideas related to visual impairment.

Language, Speech, and Hearing Services in the Schools (LSHSS). Ruth Huntley Bahr, Editor, College of Arts and Sciences, University of South Florida, 4202 East Fowler Avenue, Tampa, FL 33620. *LSHSS* is published by the American Speech-Language-Hearing Association and pertains to speech, hearing, and language services for children, particularly in schools. Articles deal with all aspects of clinical services to children, including the nature, assessment, and remediation of speech, hearing, and language disorders; program organization; management and supervision; and scholarly discussion of philosophical issues relating to school programming.

Rehabilitation and Education for Blindness and Visual Impairment (RE:View). Managing Editor, *Re:View*, Heldref Publications, 1319 18th Street N.W., Washington, DC 20036–1802. *RE:View* provides information about services for individuals with visual disabilities, including those with multiple disabilities. Articles describe useful practices, research findings, investigations, professional experiences, and controversial issues in education, rehabilitation teaching and counseling, and orientation and mobility.

Shhh Journal. This journal is published bimonthly by Self Help for Hard-of-Hearing People (SHHH). See Organizations for contact information.

Stinson, M. S., & Whitmire, K. A. (2000). Adolescents who are deaf or hard of hearing: A communication perspective on educational placement. *Topics in Language Disorders, 20*(2), 58–72. Key issues of motivation, peer relationships, and identity are examined as they pertain to adolescents with hearing impairments. These issues are discussed within the framework of the social and psychological development of adolescents who can hear, and then topics are connected to research with adolescents with hearing impairments.

The Volta Review (TVR). David F. Conway, Editor, *TVR,* Alexander Graham Bell Association for the Deaf, 3417 Volta Place N.W., Washington, DC 20007. Published quarterly by the Alexander Graham Bell Association for the Deaf, *TVR* articles address research and practical concerns for people who are deaf and hard-of-hearing.

Young, A. M., Ackerman, J., & Kyle, J. G. (2000). On creating a workable signing environment: Deaf and hearing perspectives. *Journal of Deaf Studies and Deaf Education, 5,* 186–195. This article provides an analysis of interviews with service providers (20 deaf, 21 hearing) who found that deaf and hearing individuals had differing perspectives on the integrated working experience and the use of sign language in the work setting. Deaf/hearing relations were perceived as largely person-centered by deaf individuals but as largely language-centered by hearing individuals.

ORGANIZATIONS

Alexander Graham Bell Association for the Deaf (AGBAD)

This advocacy group supports parents, children, and educational programs, and it promotes better public understanding of hearing loss, early detection, and the continued use of hearing aids. It also provides inservice training activities for teachers. AGBAD encourages people who are deaf or hard-of-hearing to communicate using residual hearing, speechreading, and speech and language skills. AGBAD gathers and disseminates information and collaborates with doctors, audiologists, speech and language specialists, and educators to promote educational, vocational, and social opportunities for those with hearing loss. AGBAD also provides scholarships for students with hearing impairments to attend regular universities and colleges. AGBAD, 3417 Volta Place N.W., Washington, DC 20007. (202) 337-5220 (Voice/TTY); info@agbell.org. *www.agbell.org.*

American Council of the Blind (ACB)

ACB is an advocacy group that supports parents, children, and educational programs. It promotes awareness and activities for people with visual impairments. ACB, 1155 15th Street N.W., Suite 720, Washington, DC 20005. (202) 467-5081; (800) 424-8666. *www.acb.org.*

American Foundation for the Blind (AFB)

AFB is a leading resource for people with visual impairments, the organizations that serve them, and the general public. A nonprofit organization founded in 1921, AFB was recognized as Helen Keller's cause in the United States. Its mission is to enable people who are blind or those with low vision to achieve equality of access and opportunity that will ensure freedom of choice in their lives. AFB, 11 Penn Plaza, Suite 300, New York, NY 10001. (800) AF-BLIND (hotline); (800) 232-3044; afbinfo@afb.org. *www.afb.org*

American Society for Deaf Children (ASDC)

Founded in 1967, the ASDC is made up of parents and families that advocate for better treatment in education and the community for children who are deaf or hard-of-hearing. ASDC,

P.O. Box 3355, Gettysburg, PA 17325. (800) 942-2732 (Voice/TTY); (717) 334-7922 (T/TTY); asdc1@aol.com. *www.deafchildren.org.*

American Speech-Language-Hearing Association (ASHA)

ASHA is an association composed of professionals in the speech and hearing science fields. The Web site provides a list of professionals for the public. ASHA, 10801 Rockville Pike, Rockville, MD 20852. (301) 897-5700 (Voice/TTY); (800) 638-8255 (Helpline); actioncenter@asha.org. *www.asha.org.*

Association for Education and Rehabilitation of the Blind and Visually Impaired (AER)

AER works to improve educational and rehabilitative services provided to people with blindness and visual impairments. AER provides information and promotes better public understanding of vision problems through publications (e.g., *RE:View, AER Report*) and other resources. AER, 206 N. Washington Street, Alexandria, VA 22314.

Blind Children's Center

Founded in 1938, this center caters to families and children from birth to school age by providing support services and education and by supporting research in the field of vision impairment. Blind Children's Center, 4120 Marathon Street, Los Angeles, CA 90029–0159. (323) 664-2153; (800) 222-3566; info@blindcntr.org. *www.blindchildrenscenter.org.*

Division for Children With Communication Disorders (DCCD)

A division of the Council for Exceptional Children, formally affiliated in 1964, DCCD is dedicated to improving the education and welfare of children with hearing, speech, and language disorders. Members receive the *Journal of Childhood Communication Disorders* and the *DCCD Newsletter* twice a year. CEC, 1100 North Glebe Road, Suite 300, Arlington, VA 22201–5704.

Division on Visual Impairments (DVI)

A division of the Council for Exceptional Children, formally affiliated in 1954, DVI promotes appropriate educational programs for individuals with visual disabilities as well as greater understanding of their concomitant life experiences. DVI has about 1,000 members and provides outlets for the exchange of ideas through a variety of resources, including the *DVI Quarterly.* CEC, 1100 North Glebe Road, Suite 300, Arlington, VA 22201–5704.

Laurent Clerc National Deaf Education Center & Clearinghouse

This Center is mandated by Congress to improve education for those who are deaf or hard-of-hearing from birth through age 21. KDES PAS-6, Gallaudet University, 800 Florida Avenue N.E., Washington, DC 20002–3695. (202) 651-5051 (Voice); (202) 651-5052 (TT); clearinghouse.infotogo@gallaudet.edu. *http:// clerccenter.gallaudet.edu/infotogo/index.html.*

National Association for Parents of the Visually Impaired, Inc.

This association provides information, resources, and support to parents whose children are visually impaired. National Association for Parents of the Visually Impaired, Inc., P.O. Box 317, Watertown, MA 02472–0317. (617) 972-7441; (800) 562-6265; napvi@perkins.pvt.k12.ma.us. *www.spedex.com/napvi.*

National Association for the Deaf (NAD)

NAD was founded in 1880 by deaf leaders who were concerned that deaf people were not included in the decision- and policy-making processes affecting their lives. NAD's mission is to assure that a comprehensive, coordinated system of services is accessible to Americans who are deaf or hard-of-hearing, enabling them to achieve their maximum potential through increased independence, productivity, and integration. Membership includes deaf, hard-of-hearing, and hearing adults; parents of deaf and hard-of-hearing children; professionals who work with deaf and hard-of-hearing children and adults; and organizations of, for, and by deaf and hard-of-hearing people. NAD, 814 Thayer Avenue, Silver Springs, MD 20910.

National Association for Visually Handicapped (NAVH)

This association provides aid for those with partial vision loss, help that will allow them to lead a life with as little disruption as possible. NAVH, 22 West 21st Street, Sixth Floor, New York, NY 10010. (212) 889-3141; staff@navh.org. *www.navh.org.*

National Braille Association, Inc. (NBA)

The NBA offers transcription services for braille readers and courses for braille transcribers. NBA, 3 Townline Circle, Rochester, NY 14623. (716) 427-8260; nbaoffice@compuserve.com. *www .nationalbraille.org.*

National Braille Press

Founded in 1927, National Braille Press is a printing and publishing house that promotes braille as the main means of literacy for a person without sight. National Braille Press, 88 St. Stephen Street, Boston, MA 02115. (617) 266-6160; (800) 548-7323; orders@nbp.org. *www.nbp.org.*

National Eye Institute (NEI)

Founded by Congress in 1968, the NEI conducts and supports research in hopes of preventing and treating vision disorders.

National Institutes of Health, U.S. Department of Health & Human Services, 2020 Vision Place, Bethesda, MD 20892–3655. (301) 496-5248; 2020@nei.nih.gov. *www.nei.nih.gov.*

National Federation of the Blind (NFB)

This advocacy group supports parents, children, and educational programs with publications and other media. Part of its mission is to improve the position in society of people who are blind. NFB, 1800 Johnson Street, Baltimore, MD 21230. (410) 659-9314; nfb@nfb.org. *www.nfb.org.*

National Information Center for Children and Youth With Disabilities (NICHCY)

NICHCY is the national information center that provides information on disabilities and disability-related issues. It has many publications in English and Spanish. NICHCY, P.O. Box 1492; Washington, DC 20013; (800) 695-0285 (Voice/TTY); nichcy@aed.org. *www.nichcy.org.*

National Information Center on Deafness (NICD)

NICD provides information on hearing impairments and assistive technology for people who are deaf or hearing impaired. It publishes fact sheets and other materials for parents, families, teachers, and other professionals. NICD, Gallaudet University, 800 Florida Avenue N.E., Washington, DC 20002.

National Institute on Deafness & Other Communication Disorders Clearinghouse (NIDCD)

Founded in 1988, the NIDCD is part of the National Institutes of Health. The NIDCD supports research and research training for all communication disorders. NIDCD, 31 Center Drive, MSC 2320, Bethesda, MD 20892–2320. (800) 241-1044 (Voice); (800) 241-1055 (TT); nidcdinfo@nidcd.nih.gov. *www.nidcd.nih.gov.*

National Library Service for the Blind & Physically Handicapped

This is a service of the Library of Congress that lends braille and audio materials to those with visual impairments. Library of Congress, 1291 Taylor Street N.W., Washington, DC 20542. (202) 707-5100; (202) 707-0744 (TTY); nls@loc.gov. *www.loc.gov/nls*.

Prevent Blindness America

Founded in 1908, Prevent Blindness America promotes eye health and safety through vision screening, influencing public policy, and supporting education and research. Prevent Blindness America, 500 E. Remington Road, Schaumburg, IL 60173. (847) 843-2020; (800) 221-3004; info@preventblindness.org. *www.prevent blindness.org*.

Self Help for Hard-of-Hearing People (SHHH)

Founded in 1979, SHHH works to allow those that are hard-of-hearing to participate fully in society. SHHH, 7910 Woodmont Avenue, Suite 1200, Bethesda, MD 20814. (301) 657–2248 (Voice); (301) 657-2249 (TT); national@shhh.org. *www.shhh.org*.

The Foundation Fighting Blindness

Founded in 1971, the Foundation Fighting Blindness funds research related to retinal degenerative diseases. The Foundation Fighting Blindness, 11435 Cronhill Drive, Owings Mills, MD 21117–2220. (888) 394–3937; (800) 683-5551 (TTY); (410) 568-0150; (410) 363-7139 (TTY); info@blindness.org. *www.blindness.org*.

References

Americans With Disabilities Act, Pub. L. No. 101-336, 104 Stat. 327 (1990).

Antia, S. D., & Kreimeyer, K. H. (2001). The role of interpreters in inclusive classrooms. *American Annals of the Deaf, 146,* 355–365.

Asch, A. (1989). Has the law made a difference? What some disabled students have to say. In D. Lipsky & A. Gartner (Eds.), *Beyond separate education: Quality education for all* (pp. 181–205). Baltimore: Brookes.

Barraga, N. C., & Erin, J. N. (1992). *Visual handicaps and learning* (3rd ed.). Austin, TX: Pro-Ed.

Byrnes, L. J., & Sigafoos, J. (2001). A "consumer" survey of educational provisions for deaf and hard of hearing students. *American Annals of the Deaf, 146,* 409–419.

Chang, S. C., & Schaller, J. (2002). Views of students with visual impairments on the support they received from teachers. *Journal of Visual Impairment and Blindness, 96,* 558–575.

Corn, A., & Ryser, G. (1989). Access to print for students with low vision. *Journal of Visual Impairment and Blindness, 83,* 340–349.

Crittenden, J. B. (1993). The culture and identity of deafness. In P. V. Paul & D. W. Jackson (Eds.), *Toward a psychology of deafness: Theoretical and empirical perspectives* (pp. 215–235). Boston: Allyn & Bacon.

D'Allura, T. (2002). Enhancing the social interaction skills of preschoolers with visual impairments. *Journal of Visual Impairment and Blindness, 96,* 576–584.

Education for All Handicapped Children Act, Pub. L. No. 94-142, 89 Stat. 773 (1975).

Fazzi, D. L., & Pogrund, R. L. (2002). *Early focus: Working with young children who are blind or visually impaired and their families.* New York: American Federation for the Blind Press.

Gallaudet Research Institute. (2001, January). *Regional and national summary report of data from the 1999–2000 annual survey of deaf and hard-of-hearing children and youth.* Washington, DC: Author, Gallaudet University.

Humphries, T. (1993). Deaf culture and cultures. In K. M. Christensen & G. L. Delgado (Eds.), *Multicultural issues in deafness* (pp. 3–15). White Plains, NY: Longman.

Individuals With Disabilities Education Act: Final Regulations, 20 U.S.C. § 300.7 (1997).

Individuals With Disabilities Education Improvement Act, Pub. L. No. 108-446, 118 Stat. 2647 (2004).

Koestler, F. (1976). *The unseen minority: A social history of blindness in the United States.* New York: McKay.

Lieberman, L., & Stuart, M. (2002). Self-determined recreational and leisure choices of individuals with deaf-blindness. *Journal of Visual Impairment and Blindness, 96,* 724–735.

Luckner, J. L., & Carter, K. (2001). Essential competencies for teaching students with hearing loss and additional disabilities. *American Annals of the Deaf, 146,* 7–15.

Luckner, J. L., & Muir, S. (2001). Successful students who are deaf in general education settings. *American Annals of the Deaf, 146,* 435–446.

Luetke-Stahlman, B., & Luckner, J. (1991). *Effectively educating students with hearing impairments.* White Plains: NY: Longman.

Moores, D. (1987). *Educating the deaf: Psychology, principles, and practices* (3rd ed.). Boston: Houghton Mifflin.

Moores, D. (2001). *Educating the deaf: Psychology, principles, and practices* (5th ed.). Boston: Houghton Mifflin.

Moores, D. F., Jatho, J., & Creech, B. (2001). Issues and trends in instruction and deafness: *American Annals of the Deaf, 1996 to 2000. American Annals of the Deaf, 146,* 72–76.

National Association of the Deaf. (2000). *Legal rights: The guide for deaf and hard of hearing people* (5th ed.). Washington, DC: Gallaudet University Press.

Newland, T. E. (1986). Children with auditory and visual impairment. In R. Brown & C. Reynolds (Eds.), *Psychological perspectives on childhood exceptionality: A handbook* (pp. 556–589). New York: Wiley.

Orr, A. L., & Rogers, P. A. (2002). *Solutions for success: A training manual for working with people who are visually impaired.* New York: American Federation for the Blind Press.

Paul, P. V., & Jackson, D. W. (1993). *Toward a psychology of deafness: Theoretical and empirical perspectives.* Boston: Allyn & Bacon.

Peavey, K. O., & Leff, D. (2002). Social acceptance of adolescent mainstreamed students with visual impairments. *Journal of Visual Impairment and Blindness, 96,* 808–812.

Schrier, E. M., Leventhal, J. D., & Uslan, M. M. (1991). Access technology for blind and visually impaired persons. *Technology and Disability, 1*(10), 19–23.

Singleton, P. (1992). We can! Empowerment of people who are deaf . . . An empowerment agenda for the 1990s and beyond. *OSERS News in Print, 5*(2), 12–15.

U.S. Department of Education. (1993). *Fifteenth annual report to Congress on the implementation of the Individuals With Disabilities Education Act.* Washington, DC: Author.

U.S. Department of Education. (1999). *Twenty-first annual report to Congress on the implementation of the Individuals With Disabilities Education Act.* Washington, DC: Author.

U.S. Department of Education. (2000). *Twenty-second annual report to Congress on the Implementation of the Individuals With Disabilities Education Act.* Washington, DC: Author.

U.S. Department of Education. (2001). *Twenty-third annual report to Congress on the implementation of the Individuals With Disabilities Education Act.* Washington, DC: Author.

U.S. Department of Education. (2002). *Twenty-fourth annual report to Congress on the implementation of the Individuals With Disabilities Education Act.* Washington, DC: Author.

Uslan, M. M. (1993). A review of two low-cost closed-circuit television systems. *Journal of Visual Impairment and Blindness, 87,* 310–313.

Index

Note: Numbers in **Bold** followed by a colon [:] denote the book number within which the page numbers are found.